As one of the world's longest established and best-known travel brands, Thomas Cook are the experts in travel.

For more than 135 years our guidebooks have unlocked the secrets of destinations around the world, sharing with travellers a wealth of experience and a passion for travel.

Rely on Thomas Cook as your travelling companion on your next trip and benefit from our unique heritage.

Thomas Cook **traveller** guides

BALTIC CRUISING
Jon Sparks

D0067342

Thomas Cook

Written and updated by Jon Sparks
Original photography by Jon Sparks

Published by Thomas Cook Publishing
A division of Thomas Cook Tour Operations Limited
Company registration no. 3772199 England
The Thomas Cook Business Park, Unit 9, Coningsby Road,
Peterborough PE3 8SB, United Kingdom
Email: books@thomascook.com, Tel: + 44 (0) 1733 416477
www.thomascookpublishing.com

Produced by Cambridge Publishing Management Limited
Burr Elm Court, Main Street, Caldecote CB23 7NU
www.cambridgepm.co.uk

ISBN: 978-1-84848-388-0

First edition © 2009 Thomas Cook Publishing
This second edition © 2011 Thomas Cook Publishing
Maps © Thomas Cook Publishing/PCGraphics (UK) Limited

Series Editor: Karen Beaulah
Production/DTP: Steven Collins

Printed and bound in Spain by GraphyCems

Cover photography © imagebroker.net/SuperStock

Contents

Introduction

The Baltic is only just a sea. It could easily be the world's largest lake. Its salinity is low, the tides are barely perceptible, and it's almost completely landlocked. In fact you could, if you wanted to, drive right round it without ever boarding a ferry. But in order to truly appreciate a region like the Baltic, where water has been the main highway for millennia, the traveller must put to sea.

Cruising is not just a fine way to see the region; it is arguably the only way. Nine countries have a Baltic shoreline: Poland, Germany, Denmark, Sweden, Finland, Russia, Estonia, Latvia and Lithuania, and it's no coincidence that five of them have their capitals on the Baltic too. Certainly there is no better, more fitting way to arrive in Stockholm or Helsinki or Tallinn than by sea. Norway is included in this guide as well; though it is not strictly a Baltic nation, many cruises visit there as part of the Baltic cruise experience. Cruising, above all, reminds us that these nations are not separated by the waters of the Baltic, but joined.

If cruising is a great way to see the Baltic, it's equally true that the Baltic is a great place to go cruising. Sea passages are short, often dispensed with overnight; if not, they are frequently enlivened by the sight of other ships, or by seemingly innumerable islands. The journey from Mariehamn to Turku is the definitive archipelago voyage.

You *will* lose count. For the neophyte and the nervous, these short passages are not the only plus point. Even the worst sailor is rarely seasick in the Baltic; there may be waves, but never the great nausea-inducing ocean swells.

Of the countries that surround the Baltic Sea, all have seen turbulent times. Borders and allegiances have changed frequently, as recently as less than two decades ago. History is fresh here, and vivid. If its vicissitudes are sometimes bewildering to contemplate, what's easier to grasp is the outstanding cultural and architectural heritage they have left in their wake, from great fortresses such as Suomenlinna in Helsinki and the Peter and Paul Fortress in St Petersburg, to the great mercantile and domestic buildings of the Hanseatic period in ports such as Visby and Tallinn.

Historic cities may be the key ports of call, but the Baltic is not overall a highly urbanised region; many of its bounding lands are sparsely populated. Wild coasts and vast inland wildernesses are equally part of the story. Through most of the region, even city-dwellers retain a strong attachment to nature, and most of the Baltic nations are now in the forefront of environmental protection. Even in the great ports, the water is often clean enough to swim in.

Natural beauty and sumptuous history; a new nation after almost every passage; and, in summer, a sun that only sets for an hour or two: these are just a few of the many delightful surprises that the Baltic has to offer.

The view from Suomenlinna towards Eteläsatama (South Harbour) and the Lutheran Cathedral, Helsinki

The Baltic region

The great geographical fact about the Baltic is how far north it is. Its southernmost extent is around 53.5° N near Wismar in Germany, and also near the German–Polish border; this is similar to northern England, or Edmonton in Canada. The northernmost part of the Gulf of Bothnia reaches about 65.5° N, equivalent to central Alaska. The Baltic is generally quite shallow, averaging little more than 50m (165ft), but reaching over 450m (1,476ft) at its deepest. Its area is approximately 375,000sq km (145,000sq miles).

In this northern region the last Ice Age, in geological terms, is only just over. Norway still has ice caps and Sweden retains a few small glaciers. The impact of glaciation dominates the natural landscape. Around the Baltic what we see is mostly the work of a great continental ice sheet, rather than the

The shoreline at Rocca al Mare, Tallinn

valley glaciers that excavated the fjords of western Norway. To generalise, in the northern part of the region, glacial erosion dominated; the ice ground and plucked at the land, and exposures of scoured rock are still common. The Scandinavian peninsula (Norway and Sweden) has the most mountainous and rugged landscapes, especially in Norway. In Sweden, Russia and, above all, Finland, thousands of irregularly shaped lakes stipple the landscape and, like a negative image, the waters of the Baltic are profusely flecked with islands.

Further south, the processes of deposition become more significant. As the ice sheets dumped their burdens of rock and silt, they left a landscape of smoother contours, with great plains relieved occasionally by low rounded hills, as in much of northern Germany, Poland and the Baltic republics. These lands are often fertile and in many areas intensively farmed.

The colossal weight of the ice depressed the land beneath; as the ice

Ships at Sjökvarteret, Mariehamn, Åland Islands

retreated, it slowly rebounded – and is still doing so; in the far north at a rate of a centimetre a year. Over time these effects turn islands into peninsulas and cause harbours to dry up (for example, at Visby; *see pp38–9*).

Initially, the Baltic was linked to the North Sea through what is now central Sweden, but as the land rose this connecting route was blocked; it is today marked by the great lakes Vänern, Vättern and Mälaren and crossed by the Göta Canal. The sea subsequently found new outlets further south, creating the islands of Denmark.

The northern position of the Baltic is also felt in its climate (*see pp126–7*), and in extreme variations in the duration of daylight. It does not quite meet the Arctic Circle, so nowhere on the Baltic coast experiences true 'midnight sun', or complete winter darkness, but at midsummer in Helsinki – the world's most northerly metropolis, and the northernmost port for most cruises – the sun dips only briefly below the horizon and there's no real darkness.

If the boundaries between land and sea are unfixed, the same has long been true of national boundaries in the region. With changes occurring as recently as 1991, it would be foolhardy to suggest that today's boundaries are permanent. However, there is some sense of stability in that national boundaries now, at least roughly, correspond with the ten main languages. That's not to say that there are no disgruntled minorities in the region, but at least one can no longer point to the wholesale suppression of nationalist aspirations.

The great political faultline that was the Iron Curtain no longer exists, and

The Baltic region

Typical scenery in the Åland Islands

it's now much harder to say where Western Europe ends and Eastern Europe begins. The reunification of Germany, political renaissance in Poland and independence for the Baltic republics mean that the southern shores of the Baltic are no longer part of the Soviet bloc. In fact all of these lands are now in the European Union. The only nations that are not are Norway, which has very close links in all sorts of other ways to the EU, and Russia, which retains its own political and economic independence.

It should be mentioned that a detached exclave of Russian territory, Kaliningrad Oblast, exists on the coast between Poland and Lithuania. The port of Kaliningrad (formerly Königsberg) is the headquarters of the Russian Baltic Fleet and the area is heavily militarised. A modest tourist traffic is developing, but as yet it is not a significant cruise port.

Within the region, certain countries have particularly close associations, especially the Nordic nations of Denmark, Sweden, Norway and Finland, which have much in common historically and culturally; the languages of Denmark, Sweden and Norway are closely related too ('Scandinavia' does not, strictly speaking, include Finland). The three Baltic republics – Lithuania, Latvia and Estonia – also have strong commonalities. Estonia also has close and developing links with Finland, based on linguistic and ethnic ties as well as geographical proximity. Finland has significant links with Russia, and Russian tourists and shoppers bring much trade to Helsinki.

History

c. 10,000 BC	First settlers arrive as ice sheets recede.
c. 1800–500 BC	Bronze Age: Baltic trade develops.
c. AD 800–1050	Vikings spread far afield. Late Vikings become Christian.
1157	Start of Swedish rule in Finland.
14th century	Rise of the Hanseatic League.
1385	Union of Krewo unites Poland and Lithuania.
1397	Union of Kalmar unites Norway, Sweden and Denmark under one crown.
16th century	The Reformation begins in Germany.
1523	Sweden throws off Danish rule; Gustav Vasa is king.
1611–1720	Frequent wars between Denmark and Sweden.
1648	Thirty Years' War ends; and Polish–Lithuanian Commonwealth dominates Eastern Europe.

1700–21	Northern War: Russian gains in eastern Baltic.
1703–12	St Petersburg founded by Peter I (Peter the Great); becomes Russia's capital.
1772–95	Partition of Poland by Russia, Prussia and Austria. Dissolution of Polish–Lithuanian union.
1803–15	The Napoleonic Wars.
1807–9	War between Russia and Sweden; Russia gains Finland.
1812	Napoleon invades Russia, makes disastrous retreat.
1814	Denmark cedes Norway to Sweden.
1815	Napoleon defeated. Realignment of European powers. National Romantic movements.
1818	Jean-Baptiste Bernadotte becomes King of Sweden.
1871	Unification of Germany.
1905	Independence for Norway. First Russian Revolution.

1914–18	World War I. Scandinavia remains neutral. St Petersburg is renamed Petrograd.	**1945– c. 1953**	Partisans in Baltic States resist Soviet rule.
		1949	Division of Germany.
1917	Revolutions in Russia.	**1953**	Death of Stalin.
1917–20	Finland and Baltic States gain independence.	**1957**	Formation of the EEC, forerunner of the EU.
1922	Creation of the USSR (Union of Soviet Socialist Republics).	**1973**	Denmark joins the EEC.
		1980	Formation of Solidarność (Solidarity) in Poland, led by Lech Wałęsa.
1924	Death of Lenin: Petrograd is renamed Leningrad.		
		1985	Accession of Mikhail Gorbachev in Soviet Union. Loosening of the Soviet empire.
1939	Molotov–Ribbentrop (Nazi–Soviet) Pact: Germany and USSR agree to divide Eastern Europe.		
		1989	Revolutions across Eastern Europe; Berlin Wall falls.
1939	Germany invades Poland; start of World War II.		
		1990	Reunification of Germany.
1939–40	Finland resists Soviet attack: the Winter War.	**1991**	Dissolution of the Soviet Union. St Petersburg reassumes its original name.
1940	Germany invades Denmark and Norway. Sweden is neutral. USSR annexes the Baltic States.		
		1995	Finland and Sweden join the EU.
1941–4	Germany breaks the 1939 pact and attacks USSR. Siege of Leningrad.	**2005**	Poland, Lithuania, Latvia and Estonia join the EU.
		2011	Turku and Tallinn are joint European Capitals of Culture.
1941–5	Germany occupies the Baltic States.		

Politics

The 20th century's tectonic shifts in world politics have often centred on Europe, and particularly on Germany and Russia. It's been said that World War I was essentially a family quarrel between great interrelated imperial dynasties. Be that as it may, its aftermath saw the fall of most of these dynasties, the accession of the Bolsheviks (later Communists) in Russia, and ultimately led to the rise of the Nazis in Germany.

World War II saw fighting rage in every nation around the Baltic, excepting Sweden. For almost 50 years thereafter, the Iron Curtain divided Europe. All this, and more, forms the background to contemporary politics around the Baltic.

More recent political upheavals are still fresh in the memory; between 1989 and 1991 the Soviet empire crumbled in a way that would have been inconceivable a few years earlier, though the rise of Solidarność (Solidarity) in Poland after 1980 and the accession of Mikhail Gorbachev in Moscow in 1985 clearly paved the way. By 1991 Poland was again a democratic state and Lithuania, Latvia and Estonia had regained the independence they had briefly enjoyed in the 1920s and 1930s. Today, eight of the ten nations featured in this book are members of the European Union, the exceptions being Russia and Norway. Norway, however, has very close associations with the EU – it is (unlike the UK) party to the

Schengen Agreement, which abolished border controls between signatories. Similarly, seven of the ten are members of NATO, the exceptions being Russia, Sweden and Finland.

Again and again, when discussing the nations of the Baltic, Russia tends to represent an exception. All of the rest can now, at least loosely, be classed as liberal democracies. Of course there are differences; for example, Denmark, Norway and Sweden are constitutional monarchies, while the others are republics. All have regular, free and fair elections and, scarcely less important, a vigorous and independent media. On the face of it, Russia, too, is a democracy and holds regular elections for the president and the Duma (Parliament). However, the Duma elections in 2007 were widely criticised. Observers from the Organisation for Security and Co-operation in Europe (OSCE) and the Council of Europe stated that there were widespread administrative abuses and, perhaps more seriously, that media coverage was heavily slanted in favour of the ruling party, United Russia, which gained 64 per cent of the vote.

Much attention centres on Vladimir Putin who, after completing two terms as president, was constitutionally obliged to stand down in May 2008. However, he was succeeded in that role by a close ally and protégé, Dmitri Medvedev. Putin himself assumed the position of prime minister, since when it is often alleged that Medvedev is little more than a puppet president and that the real power remains in Putin's hands. It must be said that Putin is genuinely popular with many Russians. After the Tsars, Lenin, Stalin and Khrushchev, many are ill at ease with the uncertainties of democracy and hanker for the certainty and stability offered by a strong leader.

While democracy appears secure in the rest of the region, memories of the Soviet era remain fresh, and throughout the Baltic region events in Russia are watched with keen interest and, sometimes, apprehension.

The Eduskunta (parliament building) in Helsinki

Politics

Culture

The swirling currents of history – trade, migration and conquest – have left multiple layers of culture almost everywhere in the Baltic. Simple national divisions are inadequate to understand this; historically one would often find ancient folk-cultures endemic among rural people, while landowners and townspeople living close by would be subject to quite different influences, even speaking a different language to their neighbours.

The rise of National Romantic movements in the 19th century can be seen as an effort by intellectuals to reconnect with endemic cultures of their own lands. This is exemplified by the work of Elias Lönnrot in Finland, who compiled and synthesised folk tales, songs and poems into an epic poem, the *Kalevala*, which played a powerful role in defining Finnish national identity.

In the 20th century, and especially under Stalin, the arts in the Soviet Union (which then included the Baltic States) were subjugated by ideological influences and only 'approved' themes were allowed. Some, like the composer Dmitri Shostakovich (1906–75), struggled to achieve expression within the system; others found it only by escaping to the West. For a shorter time, Nazi rule in Germany also grossly distorted the progress of the arts.

Today, then, the cultures of the Baltic region are richly multilayered, replete with contrasts, contradictions and occasional clashes. Yet another layer is added by imported influences, perhaps most graphically demonstrated in the part played by Italian and other foreign architects in the development of St Petersburg. Today, global influences – from MTV to Bollywood – are apparent everywhere, but at the same time, and perhaps especially in Russia and the Baltic States, there is a flowering of renewed interest in ancient traditions.

Art and architecture

In conventional histories of art, most of the Baltic nations are relegated to relatively minor roles. Germany is the great exception, but even there the key centres lay further south, not on the Baltic coast. One painter who is strongly associated with the Baltic is the great Romantic, Caspar David Friedrich (1774–1840). Born in Pomerania (then under Swedish rule), he also studied in Copenhagen. Perhaps his best-known explicitly Baltic work is *Chalk Cliffs on Rügen*. The greatest Scandinavian, if not strictly Baltic, painter is Edvard

A sculpture in Vigelandsparken, Oslo

Munch (1863–1944): poster prints of his most famous work, *The Scream*, adorn many bedroom walls, and it is an unofficial emblem of Oslo.

In sculpture, St Petersburg has a mind-boggling assemblage of monumental pieces, both from the Tsarist period (many by Italian artists) and from the Soviet era; perhaps the greatest of these is the *Monument to the Heroic Defenders of Leningrad*, a short walk from Moskovskaya metro station. The Vigeland sculpture park (*see p121*) in Oslo is a great humanistic achievement.

Norwegian stave churches are among the loveliest expressions of a great wood-building tradition. From the 19th century onwards, the Nordic nations have achieved global influence, significant in the fields of architecture and design, but their traditions go back much further. Today, new opera houses in Copenhagen and Oslo (*see pp107 and 120–21*), and KUMU in Tallinn (*see pp80–81*), demonstrate spectacularly that this tradition is alive and well.

Theatre

Many great dramatists have come from the Baltic nations: Henrik Ibsen (1828–1906) in Norway, August Strindberg (1849–1912) in Sweden, Anton Chekhov (1860–1904) in Russia. Though Strindberg spent much of his life abroad, he returned to his native Stockholm in later years.

Music

Russia has produced many great composers, and all of them passed through St Petersburg at some point. In particular, Pyotr Ilyich Tchaikovsky (1840–93) studied in the city and worked there for much of his life.

Culture

JEAN SIBELIUS

There are many 'national composers', but no one has been more deeply influential in shaping the soul of a nation than Jean Sibelius (1865–1957) in Finland. Ironically his first language was Swedish, but Sibelius and his music were steeped in the legends of the Finnish epic the *Kalevala*, as well as the more abstract influence of the Finnish landscape. His stirring *Finlandia* hints at the influence of Tchaikovsky on his music; it was an instant hit, but under Russian rule it was performed under the innocuous title *Impromptu*. His lasting reputation rests above all on seven stirring symphonies and a dazzling violin concerto.

While Edvard Grieg (1843–1907) is more associated with western Norway, the Dane Carl Nielsen (1865–1931) is a true Baltic figure: born on the island of Fyn, he worked most of his life in Copenhagen. His best-known symphony is his fourth, known as *The Inextinguishable*. And on a somewhat different plane, who can mention Sweden without thinking of ABBA?

For the significance of song in the Baltic republics, *see pp84–5*.

Cinema

The Baltic can claim at least two giants of world cinema. Sergei Eisenstein (1898–1948) is widely held to be the first director to develop a uniquely cinematic vision. Born in Rīga, he studied engineering in St Petersburg, before moving into theatre and then film. He is probably best known for the hugely influential *Battleship Potemkin* (1925).

Swede Ingmar Bergman (1918–2007) is equally revered for taking cinema into new, often introspective realms, but it should not be forgotten that he was also a great director in theatre and opera. Born in Uppsala, Bergman later settled and often worked on the tiny island of Fårö (*see p38*).

Literature

Lübeck-born Thomas Mann (1875–1955) won the 1929 Nobel Prize for his novel *Buddenbrooks*; though never named, Lübeck is clearly the setting of this epic tracing the decline of a merchant family. His brother Heinrich was also a writer, and both were prominent anti-Nazis.

Russian writers

The 2007 Nobel Laureate in Literature, Doris Lessing, cites 'the great Russians' as

Ny Carlsberg Glyptotek, a major art and sculpture gallery in Copenhagen

Statue of Henrik Ibsen outside the National Theatre, Oslo

key literary influences. Notwithstanding dramatists like Anton Chekhov and poets like Aleksandr Pushkin, few would dispute that Russia's greatest contribution is in the area of the novel. The 19th century is typically seen as the Golden Age, with writers such as Nikolai Gogol, Ivan Turgenev and, above all, Fyodor Dostoevsky (author of, among other great works, *Crime and Punishment* and *The Brothers Karamazov*) and Leo Tolstoy to the fore. Tolstoy's *War and Peace* regularly tops lists of 'The Greatest Novel Ever Written'. Under the Soviet system, many writers worked with little hope of publication, among them Boris Pasternak, whose novel *Dr Zhivago* was banned in Soviet Russia, and Aleksandr Solzhenitsyn, whose fearless criticism of the Soviet prison camp system in *The Gulag Archipelago* led to his deportation to West Germany in 1974.

Folklore and legends

The epic Finnish poem *Kalevala* exerts a great influence on Finnish people; it represents a conscious attempt to produce something akin to the Norse or Viking myths and legends, which remain potent to this day (four of our seven days of the week have names derived from Norse gods). Related folklore can be traced across much of the region; in Germany, for instance, it was a large part of the inspiration for Wagner's *Ring*. Tales of elves and other not-quite human creatures are widespread. Trolls also appear widely, especially in Norway. Russian folklore is extremely rich, full of quests, sorcerers and shape-shifters; many of its stories are best known in the West through adaptations in opera (for example, Glinka's *Ruslan and Ludmila*) or ballet (Stravinsky's *Firebird*).

Festivals and events

The Baltic revels in festivals, with even the smallest destinations having a number of events. The following are only selected highlights. Finland possibly has more festivals per head of population than anywhere else, including a plethora of downright eccentric events: there are world championships in wife carrying, mobile phone throwing, sauna bathing and playing air guitar.

April
Walpurgis Night Traditionally ushers in spring and banishes winter darkness with bonfires, song and dance. Widely celebrated, with major events at – for example – Skansen in Stockholm (*30th*).

May
Copenhagen Carnival (*mid-month*).
World Village Festival, Helsinki Global music, theatre, food and so on (*late May*).

June
Old Town Days, Vanalinn, Tallinn Medieval street festival (*early in month*).
Naantali Music Festival Mostly chamber music (*early in month*).
Midsummer A key date almost everywhere, especially in Scandinavia, Finland and the Baltic States. The astronomically minded will note that the summer solstice actually occurs on 20 or 21 June, but throughout the region the celebrations are focused on St John's Day (24 June) and its Eve – another

instance of the Church hijacking a pagan festival. Celebrations usually involve staying up all night. Bonfires are popular, to alleviate the brief period of darkness. It's known by various names – for example, in Lithuania it's Rasa, Rasos or Jonines; in Latvia Jani; in Estonia Jaanipäev. Note that many museums and other attractions may be closed on one or both dates (*23–24 June*).
White Nights Festival, St Petersburg Major multi-arts festival more formally known as Stars of the White Nights Festival (*early May–July*).

July
Õllesummer (Beer Summer), Tallinn Song Festival Grounds Open-air music and beer festival (*early in month*).
National Song Celebration, Tallinn Song Festival Grounds (*early July, every five years – 2009, 2014, etc*). Youth Song and Dance Celebrations (*2011, 2016, etc*).
Latvian Song and Dance Festival, Rīga The nation's biggest event (*early July, every five years – 2008, 2013, etc*).

Warnemünde Week Major international regatta for sailors and windsurfers (*early in month*).

Copenhagen Jazz Festival (*early in month*).

Roskilde Festival A northern Glastonbury (*early in month*).

Århus International Jazz Festival (*mid-month*).

Stockholm Jazz Festival (*mid-month*).

Kotka Maritime Festival (*late in month*).

Klaipėda Sea Festival Multifaceted festival (*late in month*).

Norway Cup, Oslo The world's largest football tournament, for young people around the world (*late July–early August*).

August

Gotland Medieval Week Visby fills with monks, merchants, jesters and musicians (*early in month*).

Hanse Sail, Rostock Maritime and multi-arts festival. Around 250 sailing ships; opportunities to sail on many of them (*early in month*).

Turku Music Festival (*mid-month*).

St Dominic's Fair, Gdańsk Goes back to 1260. A wide-ranging festival that takes over the city (*most of month*).

Baltic Sea Festival, Stockholm Classical music from leading orchestras and conductors (*late in month*).

Helsinki Festival Major multi-arts festival (*late in month*).

September

Århus Festival Mixed cultural events, such as classical music, dance and film (*early in month*).

December

Nobel Peace Prize Ceremony, Oslo.

Nobel Prize Ceremony, Stockholm.

Christmas markets Most of the cities have some sort of Christmas market; two of the slightly smaller places that really go to town are Lübeck and Turku.

Folk dancing for midsummer, Seurasaari, Finland

Highlights

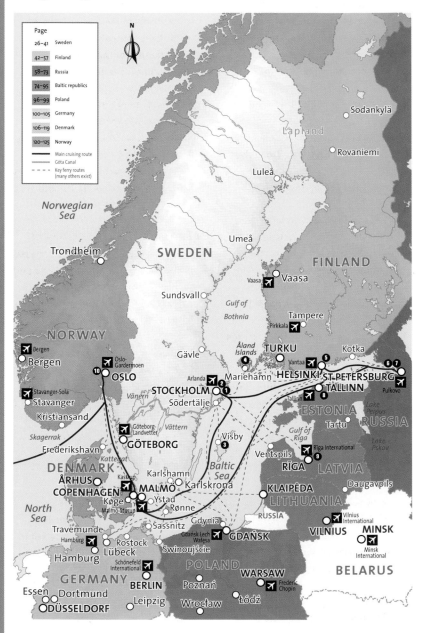

Main cruising route
Göta Canal
Key ferry routes
(many others exist)

N

Sodankylä

Rovaniemi

Lapland

Luleå

Norwegian
Sea

Umeå

Trondheim   SWEDEN   FINLAND

Vaasa   Vaasa

Sundsvall   Gulf of
Bothnia   Tampere
Pirkkala

NORWAY

Bergen
Bergen   Oslo-
Gardermoen   Gävle   Åland
Islands   TURKU   Kotka

OSLO   Vantaa
Arlanda   Mariehamn   HELSINKI   ST PETERSBURG
Stavanger-Sola   STOCKHOLM   TALLINN   Pulkovo
Stavanger   Vänern   Södertälje   Tallinn
Kristiansand   ESTONIA   Lake
Peipus   RUSSIA
Skagerrak   Göteborg-   Vättern   Tartu
Landvetter   Visby   Gulf of   Lake
Frederikshavn   GÖTEBORG   Riga   Pskov
Kattegat   Baltic   Ventspils   Riga International
DENMARK   Karlshamn   Sea   RĪGA   LATVIA
ÅRHUS   Kastrup   Karlskrona   KLAIPĖDA   Daugavpils
COPENHAGEN   MALMÖ   LITHUANIA
Køge   Ystad   Rønne   RUSSIA
North   Malmö-Sturup   Vilnius
Sea   Sassnitz   Gdynia   International
Travemünde   Gdańsk Lech   GDAŃSK   VILNIUS   MINSK
Hamburg   Rostock   Wałęsa
Lübeck   Świnoujście   Minsk
Hamburg   Schönefeld   POLAND   International
International
GERMANY   WARSAW   BELARUS
Essen   Dortmund   BERLIN   Poznań   Frederic
Chopin
DÜSSELDORF   Leipzig   Wrocław   Łódź

❶ Gamla Stan, Stockholm
Stockholm's Old Town is the largest area of medieval townscape in Europe to survive largely intact. You can easily forget you're in a modern metropolis (*see p27*).

❷ Vasamuseet, Stockholm The great ship *Vasa*, lost in the silt of Stockholm harbour for 333 years, is perfectly displayed. Probably the most stirring museum in the Baltic (*see pp31 & 33*).

❸ Visby Hanseatic Town On the peaceful island of Gotland, Visby's well-preserved Old Town allows visitors to imagine what it was like to live in the heyday of the Hanseatic League (*see pp38–9*).

❹ Down-time on the Åland Islands The red-granite islands of Åland are ideal for chilling out or for walking, cycling and sailing. Bars and restaurants are there when needed, but it's easy to find a spot where the loudest sound is the sea lapping at the rocks (*see pp56–7*).

❺ Suomenlinna, Helsinki The sprawling sea-fortress at the mouth of Helsinki harbour has mighty defences, fascinating museums and secluded corners festooned with wild flowers (*see p51*).

❻ The Hermitage, St Petersburg The Hermitage is not only one of the world's leading museums of art, but also preserves the great state rooms from the opulent court of the tsars (*see pp70–71*). It was a focal point of the October Revolution (*see p61*).

❼ Petrodvorets (Peterhof), St Petersburg Stunningly set on the shores of the Gulf of Finland, Peterhof has a great palace and one of the world's most impressive assemblages of fountains and cascades (*see pp72–3*).

❽ Vanalinn, Tallinn Tallinn's Old Town has a web of cobbled streets, several magnificent churches and Europe's best-preserved medieval Town Hall. Simply wandering here is a delight (*see pp75–81*).

❾ Art Nouveau architecture, Rīga A century ago, the exuberance and verve of Art Nouveau blew away the cobwebs of neoclassicism, and nowhere has more examples of the genre than Rīga (*see pp90–91*).

❿ Oslo's ship museums The attractive promontory of Bygdøy boasts the world's best-preserved Viking ships, the legendary Polar ship *Fram* and Thor Heyerdahl's raft *Kon-Tiki*, plus the *Gjøa*, in which Amundsen negotiated the Northwest Passage. They are not to be missed (*see pp124–5*).

Cruising routes

The Baltic is steadily growing as a cruise destination, and the market is becoming more diverse, but so far most Baltic cruises have much in common. They will nearly always visit at least four of the 'Big Five' ports (Stockholm, Helsinki, St Petersburg, Tallinn and Copenhagen). Picking the right cruise for you may involve identifying some quite subtle differences, but making sure it's the right trip for you is well worth the effort.

While the Big Five, or most of them, are nearly always on the itinerary, differences emerge both in terms of the amount of time spent at each city and as regards which other ports, if any, are also included. All of the Big Five are

major cities and tourist hotspots, with all that entails; it can make for a refreshing change of pace to visit one or two of the less obvious ports. Some, like Göteborg or Malmö, are vibrant, modern cities. At the other end of the scale are some much smaller ports, especially on the Åland Islands, Gotland or Saaremaa, ideal for getting away from it all.

A few companies offer cruises combining the Baltic with the breathtaking natural grandeur of the Norwegian fjords; these may be as short as 12–14 days. One itinerary starts in Bergen, and really only spends one day in the fjords before rounding Norway's southern coast (lovely, but less dramatic) before heading on into the Baltic, finishing in St Petersburg. An even more select few offer cruises that head north into the Gulf of Bothnia and offer a chance to see something of Lapland.

Organised cruises

The first distinction to be made is between cruises that start from a UK port and those that begin from a Baltic port.

Cruises from the UK

Starting from the UK means extra time at sea, probably the equivalent of a full day at each end of the trip. This is an important factor if your time is limited

A cruise ship moored in Oslo

The *Birka Paradise* in Stockholm

and you want to see as much of the Baltic as possible. It may be less crucial if the lifestyle of cruising itself is a big part of the attraction.

It's worth looking at which UK port the cruise starts from, though not primarily because of the difference in sailing time. Newcastle is closer than Southampton, but the time saved in travelling from a more northerly port is less than you probably expect. Where it may make a substantial difference is in your journey to and from the port. Of course, if you're based outside the UK, then it usually makes more sense to head straight for the Baltic.

Fly-cruises

A fly-cruise starts in a Baltic port, most often Copenhagen or Stockholm; you are therefore in one of the key destinations before you've even started

the cruise. This certainly appears to make better use of precious time. It remains vital to check exactly what is and isn't included in the headline price. Most obviously, does the price include flights or do you have to book these yourself? How much time does the itinerary allow in the start/finish cities? Is accommodation in these cities included or do you need to cover it yourself? How easy is it to extend your stay at either end of the cruise?

General and specialist cruises

Most cruises are aimed at a broad audience and pick their destinations and plan excursions to satisfy general interest. Particularly on a first visit to the Baltic, there's a lot to be said for this approach. However, there's a growing market for special-interest cruises; these may cater for art- or architecture-lovers,

Specialist cruises cater for many interests, including wildlife: these Barnade Geese are at Suomenlinna, Helsinki

for the musically minded, for students of history (and there's plenty of that in the Baltic!) or for bird-watchers, to name but a few. You're most likely to find out about these cruises from magazines and/or websites devoted to your special interest.

Specialist cruises may include onboard expert talks or musical performances, as well as excursions tailored to the appropriate field. It therefore makes sense to take up all or most of the excursions offered. If you're on a general cruise but still want to pursue a specific interest, you'll often be better off forgoing these excursions and making your own arrangements while on shore. In most cities this isn't difficult and usually needn't be expensive.

DIY cruises

The Baltic is criss-crossed by numerous scheduled ferry services. All but the shortest have a full range of onboard catering and, where appropriate, comfortable cabins are available. This means that there's no reason why you shouldn't create your own cruise if you prefer.

Why DIY?

The all-inclusive nature of regular cruises means that DIY cruising is not necessarily a money-saving option. DIY-ers will probably need to pay separately for meals, probably for some hotel accommodation, and often for local transport and museum admissions, all features that may be included as part of the deal on a cruise. By eating economically and using budget accommodation, you might save money, but the real benefits of choosing a DIY cruise are not necessarily economic.

One good reason for choosing this option might be if you want to spend more time in one or more of the destination ports than regular cruises allow, and perhaps to escape into the surrounding countryside. (As Stockholm and Copenhagen are turnaround ports for many cruises, stays here can easily be extended anyway.)

Another reason might be if you need, or want, to visit outside the main cruising season (which is usually May to September). Most of the ferries run all year round (*see p126*). You might want to visit some more out-of-the-way destinations, places that are not featured on most of the standard cruise itineraries. For instance, we've already mentioned the delightful islands of Åland and Gotland. Several ferries call daily at Mariehamn, on Åland, en route between Stockholm and Turku or Helsinki. Visby, on Gotland, has regular ferries from Nynashamn near Stockholm. As another way of adding variety, what about an inland cruise from Göteborg to Stockholm, by way of the Göta Canal and Sweden's two largest lakes?

The full range of available options is too broad to list here (*see pp128–9 Getting Around* for further sources of information). Practically the only major destination without an established, scheduled link by sea with other Baltic ports is St Petersburg. However, it now has a high-speed rail link with Helsinki and a good coach connection with Tallinn.

Silja Line ferry at Mariehamn, Åland Islands

Sweden

Sweden is prosperous and enviably peaceful; it was last involved in a war in 1814. Most Swedes live in vibrant cities like Stockholm, Göteborg and Malmö, but retain a deep connection to nature, and there's plenty of that to go around: lush farmland in the south, great lakes and forests, rugged mountains and the vast, near-empty spaces of Lapland.

STOCKHOLM

With nearly 2 million people, Stockholm is Scandinavia's largest metropolis, yet one is rarely far from water, space and vistas. Set between a Baltic inlet and Lake Mälaren, the city occupies 14 islands as well as chunks of the mainland. Stockholm is rich in history and culture, with over 70 museums and numerous theatres and concert halls. It has a unique global role as the home of the Nobel Prizes.

Approaches

The approach to Stockholm winds over 60km (37 miles) through the archipelago (Stockholms Skärgården; *see pp36–7*). Ships from Finland (including the Åland Islands) track the mainland coast; other traffic slips between the main archipelago and the outer skerries. The routes unite north of Vaxholm, negotiate a narrow passage and make a sharp turn starboard. A final parting of the ways takes some lines north to Värtahamnen or Frihamnen, while others enjoy classic views of the city before berthing at Södermalm. Smaller vessels may moor right in the heart of things at Skeppsbron (Stadsgården) or Nybroviken.

Skeppsbron is right next to the Royal Palace in the Old Town; Nybroviken is in the city centre, five minutes' walk from the Old Town; Båtbussana operates a regular service between the Stadsgården piers and the city centre.

Gamla Stan (Old Town)

Stockholm's Old Town centres on the island of Stadsholmen, where the city began. Its narrow streets and alleys are fascinating to explore. Stora Nygatan and Västerlånggatan, in particular, are lined with cafés, and shops with everything from pure tat to exclusive handicrafts and designer clothing.

Kungliga Slottet (Royal Palace)

The blocky Royal Palace, completed in the 1770s, is used for official functions, not as a residence. The Royal Apartments are open to visitors, who can appreciate their rococo splendour.

Slottsbacken 1, entrance on the west side. Tel: (08) 402 6130. www.royalcourt.se. Open: Jun–Aug daily 10am–5pm; Feb–mid-May & mid-Sept–early Jan Tue–Sun noon–3pm; mid–late May & early–mid-Sept daily 10am–4pm. Sometimes closed for royal occasions. Guided tours in English available. Admission charge. Metro: Gamla stan.

Livrustkammaren (the Royal Armoury) features not just armour and weaponry but coronation regalia and ornate state coaches.

Entrance on Slottsbacken. Tel: (08) 402 3030. Open: May–Jun daily 11am–5pm;

Jul & Aug daily 10am–7pm; Sept–Apr Tue, Wed & Fri–Sun 11am–5pm, Thur 11am–8pm. Admission charge.

Tre Kronor Museum reveals the remains of an earlier palace and relates its history.

Entrance on north side. Open: Hours as for the Royal Apartments.

Riddarholmen (The Knight's Islet)

Riddarholmen is actually a separate island in the Old Town, though the gap between it and the rest of Gamla Stan is largely obscured by a noisy motorway. Riddarholmen has cobbles, steps and neoclassical façades – and not a souvenir shop in sight. It is home to **Riddarholmskyrkan**, a medieval church with a 19th-century spire, burial place of Swedish monarchs and one of the classic images of Stockholm.

Riddarholmskyrkan, Riddarholmen. Tel: (08) 402 6130. www.royalcourt.se. Open: Jun–Aug daily 10am–5pm; late May & early Sept daily 10am–4pm. Closed: early Sept–late May. Admission charge. Metro: Gamla stan.

Storkyrkan (The Great Church)

The main fabric of Stockholm Cathedral (St Nicholas's Church, known as The Great Church) dates from around 1270, but interior furnishings are mostly later. The great oaken sculpture of George and the Dragon commemorates a victory over the Danes in 1471.

(Cont. on p30)

The Nobel Prizes

First awarded in 1901, the Nobel Prizes are the world's most prestigious awards. They were established by the will of Alfred Nobel (1833–96). Born in Stockholm, Nobel pursued research into explosives. He pioneered the use of nitroglycerine as an industrial explosive, but his brother Emil died in an explosion caused by this volatile substance.

Nobel strove to make nitroglycerine safer to handle. In 1866, by then based in Germany, he discovered that the admixture of diatomaceous earth produced a stable but effective explosive, which he called dynamite.

The Nobelmuseet in Stockholm

This was the basis for what became a vast industrial empire.

Although he lived mostly in France, Nobel's will stipulated that four prizes should be awarded by Swedish committees, with the Peace Prize awarded in Oslo (then part of Sweden).

The prizes

Nobel wished the prizes to be awarded to those who had 'conferred the greatest benefit on mankind'. The five original prizes were for Chemistry, Physics, Medicine, Literature and Peace. A sixth prize, for Economics, was established in 1968 by Sveriges Riksbank.

Apart from the Peace Prize, the awards are presented in Stockholm on 10 December, the culmination of 'Nobel Week'. The presentation by the king takes place at the Konserthus and is followed by a banquet at the Stadshuset (City Hall). Before 1930, the banquet venue was the Grand Hotel, where laureates traditionally stay during their time in Stockholm.

The Peace Prize is presented on the same day at Oslo Rådhuset (City Hall).

Nobel Laureates

Of the over 800 individuals who have received the Nobel Prize, so far only

The Nobels Fredssenter in Oslo celebrates Peace Prize winners

41 recipients have been women, but one of them, Marie Curie, is that rarest of beings, a double Nobel Laureate (Physics 1903, Chemistry 1911). The others are John Bardeen (Physics 1956, 1972), Fred Sanger (Chemistry 1954, 1962) and Linus Pauling (Chemistry 1954, Peace 1962). Uniquely, Linus Pauling shared neither of his prizes. Twenty organisations have received the award: the Peace Prize has gone twice to the Office of the United Nations High Commissioner for Refugees and three times to the International Committee of the Red Cross. The youngest winner of the prize to date is Lawrence Bragg, who in 1915 was awarded the Nobel Prize in Physics jointly with his father. He was just 25 years old.

For more information on the Nobel Prizes see: *http://nobelprize.org*

In Oslo, **Nobels Fredssenter** (the Nobel Peace Centre) is an inspiring celebration of the lives and work of the Peace Laureates, including Martin Luther King, Aung San Suu Kyi, Nelson Mandela and Barack Obama. *Nobels Fredssenter, Brynjulf Bulls plass 1, Rådhusplassen. Tel: (48) 30 10 00. www.nobelpeacecenter.no. Open: Jun–Aug daily 10am–6pm; Sept–May Tue–Sun 10am–6pm. Admission charge. Metro: Nationaltheateret.*

In Stockholm, the **Nobelmuseet** (Nobel Museum) tells the story of Nobel and the prizes. Artefacts from a favourite beret to a well-worn bicycle show the human side of some of the prize winners.
Nobelmuseet, Stortorget. Tel: (08) 534 81800. www.nobelmuseet.se. Open: Jun–Aug Wed–Mon 10am–6pm, Tue 10am–8pm; early–mid-Sept Wed–Mon 10am–5pm, Tue 10am–8pm; late Sept–May Wed–Mon 11am–5pm, Tue 11am–8pm. Admission charge. Metro: Gamla stan.

Trångsund. Tel: (08) 723 3016.
www.stockholmsdomkyrkoforsamling.se.
Open: May–Aug daily 9am–6pm;
Sept–Apr daily 10am–4pm.
Admission charge May–Sept.
Metro: Gamla stan.

Norrmalm

Norrmalm, on the mainland, is the site
of the modern city centre, as well as of
many of Stockholm's great 19th-
century buildings. It links to the islands
of Kungsholmen and Skeppsholmen.

Nationalmuseum (National Gallery)

Sweden's National Gallery has a great
collection of Swedish paintings, plus
some fine Dutch masters, including a
mighty Rembrandt.
Södra Blasieholmshamnen. Tel: (08) 519
54300. www.nationalmuseum.se.
Open: Wed–Sun 11am–5pm,
Tue 11am–8pm. Admission charge.
Metro: Kungstradgården.

Skeppsholmen

The island has several museums, but
it's fascinating just to wander its
waterfronts with their historic ships.
On the west side is the schooner af
Chapman and to the east you'll find
the brig Tre Kronor.
Metro: Kungstradgården.

Stadshuset (City Hall)

The noble, red-brick Stadshuset hosts
the annual Nobel Prize presentation.
The courtyards and waterfront are open
dawn till dusk; the interior is visited by

guided tours only. The tower offers
spectacular views. Lifts take you
halfway, where there's a small museum;
steps, ramps and twisting passages
finish the climb.
Hantverkargatan 1, Kungsholmen.
Tel: (08) 508 29059. Tours daily
(sometimes suspended for official events)
Jun–Aug 9.30am–4pm every 30 mins;
May & Sept 10am–3pm hourly; Oct–Apr
10am, noon. Tower open: May–Sept
daily 10am–4pm. Admission charge.
Metro: T-Centralen.

Djurgården

This area, including several key
attractions, encompasses both the
island of Djurgården itself and
adjoining parkland on the mainland,
both originally royal hunting preserves.
All is now part of Ekoparken, the
world's first urban national park.
Regular ferries run from Nybroplan
and Skeppsbrokajen; buses run along
Strandvägen; vintage trams from
Norrmalmstorg; or simply walk about
1km (²/₃ mile) from Nybroplan.

Junibacken

Behind a nondescript, shed-like
exterior, the stories of Astrid Lindgren
come to life; ride the Story Train and
visit Pippi Longstocking's Villa
Villekula. Lindgren's effigy sits quietly
just outside.
Galärvarvsvägen. Tel: (08) 587 23000.
www.junibacken.se. Open: Jul–mid-Aug
daily 9am–6pm; Jun & late Aug daily
10am–5pm; Sept–May Tue–Sun

10am–5pm. Admission charge.
Metro: Karlaplan.

Kaknästornet (Kaknäs Tower)
Standing 155m (510ft) tall, this
telecommunications tower gives
unrivalled views from its observation
deck. There's a nice café, and a gourmet
restaurant on the 28th floor.
Mörka Kroken 28–30, Ladugårdsgärdet.
Tel: (08) 667 2180. http://kaknastornet.se.
Open: Jul & Aug Mon–Sat 9am–10pm,
Sun 9am–8pm; Sept–Jun, Mon–Sat
10am–9pm, Sun 10am–6pm.
Admission charge.

Nordiska Museet (Nordic Museum)
A Gothic colossus houses a surprisingly
warm-hearted museum of cultural
history, the largest in Scandinavia.
Djurgårdsvagen 6–16. Tel: (08) 519
54600. www.nordiskamuseet.se. Open:
Jun–Aug daily 10am–5pm (Wed 8pm);

The *Vasa* is the world's only surviving 17th-
century ship

Sept–May Mon–Fri 10am–4pm (Wed
8pm), Sat & Sun 11am–5pm. Admission
charge. Metro: Karlaplan.

Skansen
Open-air museums are common now,
but this is the original, founded in
1891. Spread over the hillside are
farmsteads, homes, schools and
churches from seven centuries, and
from across Sweden. Costumed
characters are on hand in busy periods.
Enclosures house native fauna such as
reindeer, elk and bears.
Djurgården; several entrances.
Tel: (08) 442 8000. www.skansen.se.
Open: mid-Jun–Aug daily 10am–10pm;
May–mid-Jun & Sept daily 10am–8pm;
Mar, Apr & Oct daily 10am–4pm;
Nov–Feb Mon–Fri 10am–3pm, Sat &
Sun 10am–4pm. Admission charge.

Vasamuseet (Vasa Museum)
In August 1628 the mighty warship
Vasa embarked on her maiden voyage.
Within minutes she heeled to a gust of
wind and quickly sank. For centuries
she lay forgotten, before being finally
raised again after 333 years. She was
69m (226ft) long, carried 300 gunners,
and was decorated with over 700
sculptures. Vasamuseet displays her
magnificently, and enlivens every aspect
of her story.
Galärvarvsvägen 14. Tel: (08) 519 54800.
www.vasamuseet.se. Open: Jun–Aug
daily 8.30am–6pm; Sept–May Thur–Tue
10am–5pm, Wed 10am–8pm.
Admission charge. Metro: Karlaplan.

Tour: Under the bridges of Stockholm

There are many options for boat tours in Stockholm in summer (and a few year-round). This is a tour of just under two hours, which gives a good all-round view of the city, both the regular tourist haunts and the places where the people of Stockholm live, work and play. It underlines that Stockholm's watery setting is both its reason for being, and a factor that still rules its character.

Taped commentary is available in Swedish, German, Russian, Estonian, French, Spanish, Italian, Finnish, English, Chinese and Japanese. The tour starts from either Strömkajen or Nybroplan.

Leaving Strömkajen, you have the **Kungliga Slottet** (Royal Palace; *see p27*) on the right. Facing it is the city's most famous hotel, the Grand, which has played host to kings, queens, film stars including Greta Garbo, and a host of

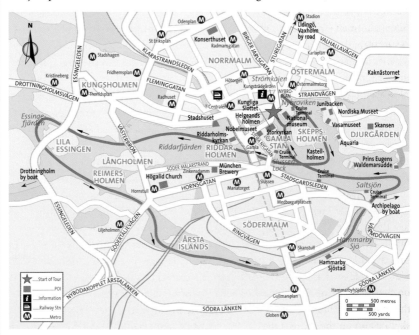

The City Hall is best viewed from the water

Nobel Prize winners. The boat slips between Blasieholmen and **Skeppsholmen** (*see p30*) to call briefly at Nybroplan, then glides past the elegant façades of Strandvägen and the multiple attractions of **Djurgården: Junibacken, Nordiska Museet, Vasamuseet,** Gröna Lund amusement park, and **Skansen** on the hill beyond (*see p31*). The boat swings round Kastellholmen and heads towards **Gamla Stan** (*see p27*) and the first lock.

The Slussen lock lurks under flyovers; the difference in water levels is less than 1m (3ft). You sail under more bridges and then the boat emerges into broad Riddarfjärden. There's a good view of **Stadshuset** (City Hall; *see p30*) on the right. On the left the towers of the **Högalid Church** dominate the skyline and on the shore is the magnificent brick edifice of the former München Brewery. Soon you're passing under Västerbron, the longest of Stockholm's many bridges. On wooded Långholmen you can glimpse a former prison, now an unusual hotel. A narrow channel takes you past the island of Lila Essingen.

Wide Essingefjärden is the turning point. The southern side of Lila Essingen has seen much redevelopment. Another narrows brings Reimersholmen close on the left, where a former distillery site is marked by a huge barrel. Twin railway bridges mark the Årsta Islands, the newer one being painted a very traditional Falu red.

The second lock lies under triple bridges. The channel widens at Hammarby Sjö. The new development of **Hammarby Sjöstad** is notable for its emphasis on sustainability. For instance, there is a deliberate policy of keeping the number of parking places to a minimum. A deep channel, with a bascule bridge, is a manmade canal, which turned the peninsula of Södermalm into an island.

You now emerge into the main harbour channel. The boat continues a short way seaward before turning for home. On the right now is Djurgården again, with the handsome **Prins Eugens Waldemarsudde** (a stately home) standing proud on a headland. There's a close view of the east shore of Gamla Stan, completely dominated by the massive Kungliga Slottet, before the trip ends back at Strömkajen.

Royal Sweden

Sweden has a long-standing and securely established monarchy. The first king of a free and united Sweden was Gustav Vasa, who was elected to the crown on 6 June 1523, after he led a campaign to overthrow Danish rule. Sweden's National Day remains 6 June. Gustav Vasa cemented his position by embracing the Protestant Reformation and taking many possessions of the Catholic Church into State hands; he also established a hereditary line.

By the end of the 17th century, Swedish power was at its height,

The changing of the guard at Kungliga Slottet

extending over Sweden, Finland, Estonia, and also possessions further south, including the area around Memel (present-day Klaipėda), Pomerania and Brandenburg. Subsequent decline culminated in the loss of Finland to Russia in 1809. This traumatic event precipitated a coup d'état, and after some unrest the Swedish Riksdag (Parliament) invited the French marshal Jean-Baptiste Bernadotte to assume the throne. At the time, the Napoleonic empire was dominant over much of Europe and it appeared prudent to adopt a monarch acceptable to Napoleon. Taking the name Karl Johan, Bernadotte ruled as regent for a few years, before taking the crown in 1818. By this time, of course, Napoleon had been defeated and the empire was crumbling, but the Bernadotte dynasty endured and is still the ruling house today.

The present king, Carl XVI Gustaf, came to the throne in 1973. The following year the country adopted a new constitution, further limiting the powers of the crown, and in 1980 the law was again changed to ensure that the eldest child would inherit, regardless of gender. The heir to the throne is Crown Princess Victoria.

Drottningholm is the real royal residence

Royal Palaces

There are ten Royal Palaces, all in the Stockholm region. The official royal residence is Kungliga Slottet (see p27), but the royal family actually live at **Drottningholm**, around 10km (6 miles) west on the shores of Lake Mälaren – and who can blame them, as this palace has all the warmth and grace that Kungliga Slottet lacks. Drottningholm is a Baroque palace, begun in 1662. It was designed by Nicodemus Tessin the Elder, but the interiors were mainly completed by his son, Tessin the Younger. Tours visit some of the most splendid apartments, but not the south wing where today's royals live.

Drottningholm. Tel: (08) 402 6280. www.royalcourt.se. Tours: May–Aug daily 11am–4.30pm; Sept daily noon–3.30pm; Oct–Apr Sat & Sun noon–3.30pm. Admission charge.

The entire estate is a World Heritage Site, including not only the palace but also the great Baroque garden, also planned by Tessin the Younger. This is currently undergoing replanting, with more than 1,000 lime trees being installed. Beyond the garden is **Kina Slott** (the Chinese Pavilion), dating from 1767.

Open: May–Aug daily 11am–4.30pm; Sept daily noon–3.30pm. Closed: Oct–Apr. Admission charge.

The surrounding English-style park is very popular with Stockholmers for picnics. Close by the palace, **Drottningholms Slottsteater** (Court Theatre) is a perfectly preserved Baroque theatre, which has fully functioning stage machinery.

Drottningholms Slottsteater. Tel: (08) 759 0406. www.dtm.se. Tours: twice hourly, May daily noon–4.30pm; Jun–Aug daily 11am–4.30pm; Sept daily 1–3.30pm. Off-season tours by appointment. Admission charge.

Sweden

Stockholms Skärgården (The Stockholm Archipelago)

Stockholm's archipelago extends around 50km (30 miles) seaward as the gull flies. It's a potentially bewildering maze of nearly 30,000 islands, islets, skerries and reefs. Almost 200 are permanently inhabited, and many more have summer homes and cabins on them. A number of the main islands are now linked to the mainland, and/or each other, by bridges.

Sightseeing tours generally cover the main fairway, largely duplicating the route that cruise ships take (see p26). Taking a local ferry instead is cheaper and arguably more authentic; you won't get the running commentary, of course, but there may be more space at the rail for viewing.

Lidingö

Purists may say that Lidingö is a 'city' island rather than part of the 'real' archipelago, and certainly it's more usual to get there by land transport. Its key attraction is **Millesgården**, the former home of the famous sculptor Carl Milles (1875–1955). Delightful terraced gardens, framing fine views over the water, are filled with Milles's work, including many fountains. Many of the pieces are replicas of originals located around the world, notably in the USA. Milles's sister Ruth was also a noted sculptor and his wife, Olga, a

Swedish summer homes are dotted around the archipelago

Vaxholms Fästning is a forbidding sight from the water

successful painter: examples of their work can also be seen.

Take the T-bana to Ropsten and then a local bus to Torsvik (one stop) or Lidingöbana train to Torsvik; from either of these it's a short, signposted, walk to Millesgården. Occasional buses (No 207) go all the way from Ropsten to Millesgården.

Herserudsvägen 32, Lidingö.
Tel: (08) 446 7580.
www.millesgarden.se. Open: mid-May–Sept daily 11am–5pm; Oct–mid-May Tue–Sun noon–5pm. Admission charge.

Vaxholm

The small town of Vaxholm is a key centre in the archipelago. It's readily accessible by land from Stockholm (T-bana to Tekniska Högskolan, then bus No 670). Yellow car-ferries shuttle almost ceaselessly across the 1km (²/₃-mile) strait to Rindö, and passenger ferries fan out to several other islands as well as linking back to Stockholm. With a busy small-boat harbour, too,

the comings and goings never let up, especially in summer – and where better to watch from than one of the pavement cafés strewn along the waterfront? The town has several galleries and craft shops. The Vaxholm Hotel is a lovely Art Nouveau building. Five minutes' walk away is the quiet 19th-century north harbour.

Across a narrow channel is **Vaxholms Fästning** (Vaxholm Fortress). Its strategic position was exploited from at least the 16th century, but most of the present imposing structure dates from the 19th. Used until 1944, it is now preserved and houses a coastal defence museum and also some novel B&B accommodation. During opening times a small ferry links it to Vaxholm and the regular ferries from Stockholm also call.

Vaxholms Fästning. Tel: (08) 591 71890.
www.vaxholmsfastning.se. Open: Jun daily noon–4pm; Jul & Aug daily 11am–5pm; early Sept Sat & Sun 11am–5pm). Admission charge.

GOTLAND

Around 160km (100 miles) long and up to 50km (30 miles) wide, Gotland is the largest island in the Baltic without a fixed link to the mainland. It is visited by a growing number of cruise ships and served by regular ferries from Oskarshamn, north of Kalmar, and Nynashamn, on the Stockholm local train network.

Gotland is largely composed of limestone, unusual in Sweden. Inland, the rock supports rich flora and the herb-rich grazing imparts a special flavour to local lamb. The 800km (500 miles) of coastline mixes steep cliffs, especially in the west, and fine beaches. There are many strange rock-stacks called *raukar*; these are remnants of coral reefs formed around 400 million years ago, when Gotland lay near the Equator. Some of the most striking are on the island of **Fårö**, a ten-minute ferry ride off the northern tip of Gotland. Fårö was beloved by the great film director Ingmar Bergman and its *raukar* formed a weird backdrop in several of his films.

South of Visby there are extensive tracts of limestone heathland, bright with flowers. Windmills break the level skylines. The Hoburgen headland has some impressive limestone formations.

Nature-lovers should not miss a trip to **Stora Karlsö** (regular boats in summer from Klintehamn), the world's second-oldest nature reserve. Highlights include great colonies of auks and an amazing variety of orchids.

Gotland has tranquil rural landscapes and wonderful beaches, but the main draw for most visitors is the historic town of Visby, a World Heritage Site.

Visby

A trading centre for over a thousand years, Visby was a key Baltic port in the days of the Hanseatic League (*see pp104–5*), and continued to thrive for several centuries afterwards. Encircled by 3.4km (2 miles) of town wall, boasting 36 towers, the town includes almost 200 buildings from the Hanseatic period, and many imposing merchants' houses from the 17th and 18th centuries. Largely traffic-free, it's a delightful place to explore. One illustration of its popularity is that Visby is said to have more restaurants for its size than anywhere else

Limestone heathland in Gotland

Visby was an important Hanseatic port

in Sweden. A good place to start is the **Information Centre**, beside the harbour. *Skeppsbron 4–6. Tel: (0498) 201 700. Open: mid-Jun–mid-Aug daily 9am–6pm; May–mid-Jun & mid-Aug–Sept Mon–Fri 8am–5pm, Sat & Sun 11am–3pm; Oct–Apr Mon–Fri 8am–4pm.*

Domkyrkan

The former harbour, Almedalen, is now a park. From here the Old Town rises up the slope, dominated by the 13th-century Domkyrkan, the only church from the Hanseatic period that remains intact (though several others stand as evocative ruins).
Domkyrkan. Tel: (0498) 206 800. Open: daily 8am–5pm.

Gotlands Fornsal

The local museum portrays 8,000 years of history. It has an equally informative exhibition on Natural Gotland, and a science-discovery centre, Fenomenalen.
Strandgatan 14. Tel: (0498) 292 700. www.gotlandsmuseum.se. Open: Jun–mid-Aug daily 10am–6pm; mid-Aug–May Tue–Sun noon–4pm. Admission charge.

Kapitelhusgården (Chapter House Yard)

Perhaps the best place to get a vivid sense of Visby's past is Kapitelhusgården (Chapter House Yard), a medieval courtyard where role-playing characters stroll in costume and you can see, and sometimes try, various crafts.
Tel: (0498) 247 637. www.kapitelhusgarden.se. Open: Jul–mid-Aug daily noon–10pm. Free admission.

GÖTEBORG (GOTHENBURG)

Sweden's second city and premier seaport, thriving Göteborg is a lively yet relaxed city; there's much to see and – as the cruise market grows – it is likely to become a more frequent destination. It could also be a good starting point for a DIY cruise, taking the Göta Canal to Stockholm.

The Old Town centres around **Gustaf Adolfs Torg**, the main city square since 1621. As befits a great port, much interest lies along the waterfront.

Gathenhielmskulturreservatet (Conservation area)

The conservation area has many wooden houses, including some from the 16th and 17th centuries.
Near the maritime museum.
Tel: (031) 612 500.

Göteborgsoperan (Opera House)

The striking, ship-like Göteborgsoperan was built in 1994. Its programme includes opera, ballet and musicals.
Christina Nilssons Gata.
Tel: (031) 131 300. www.opera.se.
Guided tours available.

Maritiman

The world's largest floating maritime museum, it is home to 19 ships.
Packhusplatsen. Tel: (031) 105 960.
www.maritiman.se. Open: May–Sept daily 10am–6pm; Apr Fri–Sun 10am–6pm; Oct Fri–Sun 10am–4pm. Closed: Nov–Feb. Admission charge.

Sjöfartsmuseet-Akvariet

A combined maritime museum and aquarium.
Karl Johansgatan 1–3. Tel: (031) 368 3550. www.sjofartsmuseum.goteborg.se. Open: Tue & Thur–Sun 10am–5pm, Wed 10am–8pm. Admission charge.

MALMÖ

Malmö, Sweden's third city, now orients itself principally to the Öresund region, a model of cross-border integration. It is, after all, only 35 minutes by train from Copenhagen. Malmö can be conveniently divided into three areas. The engaging Old Town, just inland from the railway station, surrounds the elegant Stortorget square; adjacent Lilla Torg buzzes with pavement cafés. The newer city is less picturesque but great for shopping.

Koggmuseet (Cog Museum)

Arguably Malmö's most enjoyable museum, the Cog Museum lies by the harbour. It centres on a complete, seagoing replica of a sturdy medieval trading ship or cog, and in summer the harbour yard is a lively venue for craft demonstrations and re-enactments.
Skeppsbron 10. Tel: (040) 330 800. www.medeltidsskeppen.se. Open: Jun–Aug daily 11am–4pm; Sept–May Tue–Fri 11am–4pm. Admission charge.

Malmöhus Slott (Malmö Castle)

Several museums cluster in and around Malmö Castle, a 15th-century moated fortress just west of the Old Town.

Malmöhus Slott near the Old Town

Tel: (040) 344 400. Open: Jun–Aug daily 10am–4pm; Sept–May Mon–Fri 10am–4pm, Sat & Sun noon–4pm. Admission charge.

Västrahamnen

West from the station, this is an old port/industrial quarter whose current regeneration is a beacon of sustainable practice. It is dominated by the astounding **Turning Torso**, a 190m (625ft) tower with a 90-degree twist, designed by Santiago Calatrava. The adjacent Turning Torso Gallery has shops, a 'twisted' restaurant and an **Experience Centre**, with an exciting film about the tower.
Västra Varvsgatan. Tel: (040) 357 713. www.turningtorso.se. Open: Mon–Fri 11am–6pm, Sat 11am–4pm.

KALMAR

Kalmar, on Sweden's east coast and sheltered by the island of Öland, is one of the country's most historic towns. In 1397 the Union of Kalmar united Sweden, Denmark and Norway.

For centuries, the castle, **Kalmar Slott**, was one of Sweden's most significant fortresses. The great Gustav Vasa beefed up the fortifications in the 16th century, while the interior was remodelled as a Renaissance palace.
*Tel: (480) 451 490.
www.kalmarslott.kalmar.se.
Open: Jul & Aug daily 10am–5pm;
May & Jun daily 10am–6pm; Apr & Oct
Sat & Sun 11am–3.30pm; Nov–Mar
occasional weekends 11am–3.30pm.
Admission charge.*

KARLSKRONA

The home of Sweden's navy in its days as a great power, Karlskrona's naval city is now a World Heritage Site. Don't miss the former sea-gate, Kungsbron (King's Bridge) or the attractive scene at Fisktorget, a haven for pleasure craft. For most, though, the highlight is the great naval dockyard, one of the best surviving examples in the world of a shipyard from the heyday of sail.

Finland

Ruled by Sweden for most of its recorded history, Finland fell under Russian sway in the 19th century, only attaining independence in 1919. Yet somehow the Finns have forged a strong sense of national identity, whose wellsprings include their unusual language, a challenging yet mystically beautiful environment, the folk-tales that became the Kalevala *and the music of Sibelius.*

From the start, Finland held true to democratic ideals and somehow, at great cost, this small, young nation managed to hold off first the Soviet Union and then the Third Reich. From a low base 50 years ago, Finland has become one of the world's most prosperous nations. It's little wonder that Finland has become something of a role model for the newly independent Baltic republics, especially Estonia.

HELSINKI
(SWEDISH: HELSINGFORS)

Helsinki is not just a beautiful city and it is not just one of the safest cities on earth: it is, above all, a city that works. It may be the world's most northerly metropolis, but the central districts, where most of the main attractions lie, are compact and easy to navigate, and it's never far to an open space and a view across water. It may not be the most spectacular of the Baltic cities; it is certainly not the flashiest, but give it a little time and you may just conclude that it is the most approachable of them all.

Approaches

When it comes to its sea approaches, Helsinki has few peers, with its fringe of granite islands. Most vessels dock at the

South Harbour, gliding in past the great sea fortress of Suomenlinna. Rows of lovely Art Nouveau blocks line the shore to the west; neoclassical façades announce the historic centre of the city. Above it all soar the white towers and green copper dome of the Lutheran Cathedral, an enduring symbol of the city. Most attractions are in easy walking distance, and the harbour is also a nexus for tram and bus routes.

The largest ships berth at the West Harbour, 2km (1¼ miles) from the centre. Bus 15A gives a regular link into the city centre.

Eteläsatama (South Harbour)

The arrival point for many cruise ships and ferries, this is also a local hub, with the ferry to Suomenlinna and various sightseeing boats. Beside the harbour are the bustling Kauppatori (Market Square) and the historic Kauppahalli (Market Hall) and just a stone's throw away is the main tourist information centre. Beyond a ring of tram-tracks around the much-loved Havis Amanda fountain, the narrow Esplanade Park runs into the centre of the city.

Overlooking the harbour, the red-brick **Uspenski Cathedral**, the biggest Orthodox church in Western Europe, testifies to a century of Russian rule. Designed by Aleksei Gornostajev and built between 1862 and 1868, it has 13 golden onion domes, corresponding to Christ and the Apostles. Inside, the walls are richly decorated, the centrepiece being the great gilded altar screen.

Kanavakatu 1. Tel: 0207 220 683.
Open: May–Sept Mon–Fri 9.30am–4pm,
Sat 9.30am–2pm, Sun noon–3pm;
Oct–Apr Tue–Fri 9.30am–4pm, Sat
9.30am–2pm, Sun noon–3pm. Free
admission. Metro: Rautatientori/
Kaisaniemi.

Senatintori (Senate Square)

Just a block north of Kauppatori, Senatintori's harmonious proportions embody the vision of the tsar's planner J A Ehrenström and architect C L Engel. In the centre is a monumental statue of Tsar Alexander II.

(*Cont. on p46*)

The approach to Helsinki

Walk: Essential Helsinki

This walk exemplifies Helsinki's special character. Bustling city streets alternate with peaceful waterside paths, striking architecture with open vistas, street-life with wildlife. In distance, the walk is quite short; actual walking time should be no more than 1½ hours. However, with so much to see, it could easily fill a whole day.

Start at Eteläsatama (South Harbour), beside Kauppahalli market hall.

Walk north beside the harbour to **Kauppatori** (*see p43*) and follow the harbour edge to the right. Overlooking Kauppatori are City Hall and the

Presidential Palace. Cross a small bridge near the Suomenlinna ferry terminal and bear left alongside a busy road. The blocky white building on the right is the Enso building, one of Alvar Aalto's more controversial creations. The

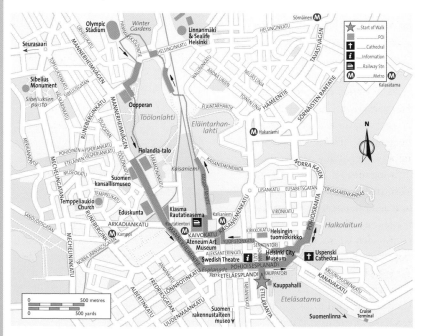

Uspenski Cathedral (*see p43*) stands on a little knoll just up to the right.

Continue to the small harbour of Halkolaituri, with its wooden boats, then backtrack almost to the Uspenski Cathedral before crossing to follow Aleksanterinkatu, which soon leads to **Senatintori** (*see p46*), dominated on its north side by the **Lutheran Cathedral** (*see p46*).

Leave the square by its northwest corner and follow Yliopistonkatu. At its end the **Ateneum Art Museum** (*see p46*) is just ahead. Then cross the street to the **Railway Station** (*see p46*).

Enter the great doors, with monumental granite figures alongside. Go right on the concourse and leave by a side exit next to platform 1. Go left down a narrow street and ahead into Kaisaniemi Park. There are some interesting sculptures made from the stumps of trees along here, and in winter there are several open-air ice rinks. You soon come to the shores of Eläintarhanlahti; it looks like a lake but it is actually an arm of the sea. Carry on gently uphill, keeping parallel to the railway line, until a bridge over it.

Swing round left, overlooking **Töölönlahti** (*see pp46–7*), which is linked to Eläintarhanlahti by a channel under the railway. There are a number of fine old wooden houses scattered along the slope here. Follow the shore round to the left a busy road (Helsinginkatu) and then cross it to reach the Winter Gardens. Bear left through these to reach the Olympic Stadium.

Kauppatori is always busy

Head back south from the stadium and re-cross Helsinginkatu. **Oopperan** (Finnish National Opera; *see p47*) stands on the corner by a large junction. You can walk in front of it along the road, but preferably take a quieter path behind. Continue heading south alongside Töölönlahti towards the white **Finlandia-talo** (*see p47*). Almost opposite Finlandia-talo, across the busy road, is the **Suomen kansallismuseo** (National Museum; *see p47*). Continue down the road to the steps of the **Eduskunta** (Parliament; *see p50*).

Keep following the road in the same direction for about 700m (765yds) to the junction with Lönnrotinkatu on the right. Opposite this is Pohjoisesplanadi, and the Swedish Theatre. Beyond the theatre you can walk down the **Esplanade Park** itself (*see p43*), or stay on Pohjoisesplanadi and visit one of its many pavement cafés. The Esplanade ends at a complex of tram tracks surrounding the Havis Amanda statue. Just beyond is Kauppatori, and the circuit is complete.

Eyes are inevitably drawn to the dazzling white Lutheran Cathedral, **Helsingin tuomiokirkko**. It was completed in 1852, 12 years after Engel's death. Above the porticoes, 12 statues, representing the Apostles, form the biggest assemblage of zinc sculptures in the world: each is 3.2m (10½ft) tall and weighs around a ton. The interior (usually entered through a door round to the left, as you come up the steps) is plain, simple and flooded with light.

On the west side of the square is the main building of the **University of Helsinki**. Opposite stands the former **Senate** building, now officially called the **Palace of the Council of State**. On the south side are the **Old Town Hall** and a row of grand houses, many now shops, galleries and restaurants.

Between Kauppatori and Senatintori, car-free **Sofiankatu** is virtually an open-air museum. Here, too, is the main collection of the **Helsinki City Museum**, exploring the history of the city.

A few minutes west of Senatintori is **Rautatientori** (Railway Square), a major interchange for bus, tram and metro, dominated by **Rautatieasema** (Railway Station), one of Saarinen's great buildings (*see p48*).

Helsingin tuomiokirkko, Unioninkatu 29. Tel: (09) 2340 6120. Open: Mon–Sat 9am–6pm, Sun noon–6pm. Free admission.

Helsinki City Museum, Sofiankatu 4. Tel: (09) 3103 6630. www.hel.fi. Open: Mon–Fri 9am–5pm, Thur 9am–7pm, Sat & Sun 11am–5pm. Free admission. Metro: Kaisaniemi.

Ateneum Art Museum

Just south of Rautatientori is Finland's largest art museum, home to most of the nation's favourite paintings.

Ateneum, Kaivokatu 2. Tel: (09) 173 361. www.ateneum.fi. Open: Tue & Fri 9am–6pm, Wed & Thur 10am–8pm, Sat & Sun 11am–5pm. Admission charge. Metro: Rautatientori.

Töölonlahti (Töölo Bay)

A little further north and west, Töölonlahti may look like a lake, but is linked to the sea. A circuit of its shores

Looking across Töölonlahti

The Oopperan on the Töölonlahti shore glows at night

passes some lovely wooden villas on the northeast side, and several major attractions are clustered around.

Closest to the water is the **Oopperan** (Opera House), designed by Eero Hyvämäki, Jukka Karhunen and Risto Parkkinen and completed in 1993. On the southwest side is **Finlandia-talo** (Finlandia Hall), one of the signature buildings of Alvar Aalto (*see pp48–9*). The exterior is clad in black granite and white marble, while the auditorium is almost completely devoid of right-angles. A new extension facing the water has just been built, opening in spring 2011.

Finlandia-talo was intended to be part of a much grander vision, a great plaza between Töölonlahti and Rautatieasema, but this has yet to be realised. Modest gardens occupy some of the space; sadly, much of the rest of it is a car park.

Just across busy Mannerheimintie is the granite tower of **Suomen kansallismuseo** (National Museum of Finland), also by Saarinen. Worth a visit for its architecture alone, its collections portray Finnish life from prehistory to the present.

Finlandia-talo, Mannerheimintie 13e.
Tel: (09) 403 241. www.finlandiatalo.fi.
Guided tours most days.
Admission charge.
Suomen kansallismuseo, Mannerheimintie
34. Tel: (09) 4050 9544.
www.nba.fi/en/nmf.
Open: Tue 11am–8pm, Wed–Sun
11am–6pm. Admission charge; free Tue
evenings. Metro: Rautatientori.

Architecture in Finland

Finland has a very special place in the history of modern architecture. Quite why this should be, is unclear: perhaps one factor is the collision of Eastern and Western influences. Also, Finland's rapid emergence into the modern world means that barely one-tenth of its buildings are over 100 years old, so Finnish architects have had more of the freedom of the blank canvas than most. The two best-known Finnish architects are Eliel Saarinen and Alvar Aalto.

Eliel Saarinen (1873–1950) studied in Helsinki and qualified in 1897, at the height of the Art Nouveau movement (*see p91*). Strongly influenced by this, not least in the integration of architecture and interior design, Saarinen and his partners

Light filters in through the windows of Saarinen's Railway Station

Gesellius and Lindgren added distinctive Finnish influences and original style. Great products of this collaboration include Hvitträsk (*see p52*), near Helsinki (completed 1903), where they had their office and private houses. In the city itself are the National Museum of Finland (*see p47*, 1910) and the Railway Station (1919), attributed principally to Saarinen.

In 1922 Saarinen came second in the competition to design the Chicago Tribune Tower and subsequently moved to the USA. His runner-up design actually proved more influential than the winner's, and was the basis of the Gulf Building in Houston, Texas. Perhaps his most important realised design in America was the Cranbrook Academy near Detroit, where he taught for many years. His son **Eero** (1910–61) became a major figure in American architecture and designed the Gateway Arch in St Louis.

Alvar Aalto (1898–1976) also studied in Helsinki, graduating in 1921. He first practised in the central city of Jyväskylä, which still has more Aalto buildings than anywhere else. Aalto began as an uncompromising functionalist, but progressively developed a more organic philosophy,

Finlandia-talo is one of Alvar Aalto's great constructions

strongly influenced by his first wife Aino, an artist herself, and by visits to the Mediterranean region. His mature style seeks to connect people, buildings and the broader environment, and makes extensive use of natural materials, in keeping with the Finnish love of nature and the outdoors. Perhaps it can be summed up as Modernism with a human face. Notable buildings include Villa Mairea in Noormarkku, in western Finland; Kulttuuritalo (House of Culture) in Helsinki, and the gorgeous Opera House in Essen, Germany. Aalto also designed the town centre of Seinajoki in Finland, and the complete town plan of Rovaniemi, close to the Arctic Circle. His last great building is **Finlandia-talo** in Helsinki (*see p47*, completed 1972), literally just across the street from Saarinen's National Museum and near the station.

While in Helsinki, architecture devotees will be drawn to **Suomen rakennustaiteen museo (Museum of Finnish Architecture)**. Or head out of town to learn more about Alvar Aalto's life and work – it's three hours by the fastest trains to Jyväskylä and the **Alvar Aalto Museum**.

Suomen rakennustaiteen museo, Kasarmikatu 24. Tel: (09) 8567 5100. www.mfa.fi. Open: Tue, Thur & Fri 10am–4pm, Wed 10am–8pm, Sat & Sun 11am–4pm. Admission charge; free Fri.

Studio Aalto, Tiilimäki 20. Tel: (09) 481 350. www.alvaraalto.fi. Open: tours only, Aug daily 11.30am; Sept–Jul Tue–Fri 11.30am. Admission charge.

Alvar Aalto Museum, Alvar Aallon katu 7, Jyväskylä. Tel: (014) 266 7113. www.alvaraalto.fi. Open: Jul & Aug Tue–Fri 10am–6pm, Sat & Sun 11am–6pm; Sept–Jun Tue–Sun 11am–6pm. Admission charge.

The Sibelius monument even makes its own music in the right weather conditions

Heading south on Mannerheimintie, one soon passes, on the right, the rather squat **Eduskunta** (Parliament); almost opposite is the elegantly curving **Kiasma** (Museum of Contemporary Art), completed in 1998, designed by the American Steven Holl. Two minutes west, amid streets of tall Jugendstil blocks, one suddenly encounters a granite outcrop topped by a low dome. This is **Temppeliaukio Church**, often referred to as the Rock Church, one of Helsinki's most popular attractions. In essence it is a roofed-in quarry, with bare rock still visible around the walls. The church has excellent acoustics and is often used for concerts. Designed by brothers Timo and Tuomo Suomalainen, it was completed in 1969.

About a ten-minute walk west of Töölonlahti (or take bus No 24) is **Sibeliuksen puisto** (Sibelius Park), a fine, natural-seeming open space. On its west side is a wonderful monument to Jean Sibelius, standing on an outcrop with a backdrop of trees. Created by Eila Hiltunen and completed in 1967, the monument is composed of over 600 welded steel pipes standing up to 8.5m (28ft) high, evoking images of organ pipes or birch trees. In high winds it even makes its own music.

From here strong walkers could continue to **Seurasaari**, or you can rejoin bus No 24. Tram No 4 also passes nearby. Seurasaari is a fine open-air museum occupying an island site that gives a broad picture of Finnish rural life over three centuries. Scattered among the trees, over 80 separate buildings include complete farmsteads, a windmill and a 300-year-old wooden church. There are regular craft demonstrations and a café and shop on site.

Temppeliaukio Church, Lutherinkatu 3. Tel: (09) 2340 5920. Open: daily from 10am (Sun 11.45am); hours vary to accommodate services and concerts. Seurasaari. Tel: (09) 4050 9660. www. nba.fi. Open: Jun–Aug daily 11am–5pm; mid-May–late May & early–mid-Sept Mon–Fri 9am–3pm, Sat & Sun 11am–5pm. Closed: mid-Sept–mid-May. Admission charge.

Suomenlinna

The ferry from Eteläsatama runs until after midnight and is a great scenic ride in itself. One of the world's largest sea fortresses, Suomenlinna is a World Heritage Site. Spreading over half a dozen islands, it incorporated a garrison, naval dockyard and support services, and still has around 900 inhabitants.

Construction began in 1748, under Augustin Ehrensvärd, but when Sweden and Russia fought over Finland in 1808, the fortress surrendered tamely. Originally called Sveaborg, it was renamed Suomenlinna (Finland's Fortress) after the declaration of independence in 1917, and was handed over to civilian use in 1973.

Much of Suomenlinna, including its great bastions, now covered in wild flowers, is open to explore freely. The site also includes seven museums and numerous galleries, studios, cafés and restaurants. The best place to start is the visitor centre, adjacent to which is the **Suomenlinna Museum and Multivision**. The 20-minute widescreen show (available in English) is a great introduction to Suomenlinna, and the rest of the museum fills in the details.

Suomenlinna. Tel: (09) 4050 9691. www.nba.fi. Open: May–Sept daily 10am–6pm; Oct–Apr daily 10.30am–4.30pm. Admission charge.

AROUND HELSINKI

Three key attractions lie in easy reach of Helsinki, but all in different directions. Ainola is a must for music-lovers, Hvitträsk for architecture buffs. Porvoo is a lovely historic town and a great place to shop for arts and crafts.

The church at Seurasaari is 300 years old

Ainola

Ainola was Sibelius's home for much of his adult life; most of the great symphonies were composed in the study upstairs, with its view over the lake, Tuusulanjärvi. Built in 1904, to the design of Lars Sonck, the house is remarkably modest and unpretentious. Many fittings were designed by Aino Sibelius, who also nurtured the garden. Aino lived on here for a decade after her husband's death, and both are buried in the garden. Around 35km (22 miles) north of Helsinki, reached by bus on the Järvenpää line, Ainola stop, with a 200m (220yd) walk; or by train to Järvenpää, then local bus or taxi.

Ainolantie, 04400 Järvenpää.
Tel: (09) 287 322. www.ainola.fi.

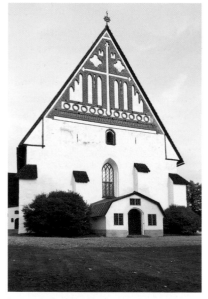
Porvoo Cathedral with its brick decoration

Open: May–Sept Tue–Fri 10am–5pm.
Admission charge.

Hvitträsk

Standing in attractive gardens near the wooded shores of Vitträskjärvi, Hvitträsk was designed by Herman Gesellius, Armas Lindgren and Eliel Saarinen (*see p48*), combining homes and studio. Now a museum to their work, the stone and log structure is the apotheosis of National Romantic architecture. Around 30km (19 miles) west of Helsinki (train to Luoma then 2.7km/1¾-mile walk, or train to Kauklahti then taxi).

Hvitträskintie 166, FI-02440 Luoma.
Tel: (09) 4050 9630. www.nba.fi.
Open: May–Sept daily 11am–6pm; Oct–Apr Tue–Sun 11am–5pm.
Admission charge.

Porvoo

Around 45km (28 miles) east of Helsinki. Regular buses run from Helsinki; in summer there are boat trips, including on a century-old steamship, and on summer Saturdays a museum train.

After Turku, Porvoo is the oldest town in Finland; unlike Turku, its Old Town is largely complete. Old Porvoo includes around 250 houses and 300 outbuildings, presently home to about 700 people. Many are of wood, often stained with red ochre. The exceptionally picturesque row of shore houses originally served as warehouses in the days of the Hanseatic League.

Many of Porvoo's wooden buildings were used for storage at the time of the Hanseatic League

Commodities included fish, wine, spices, tobacco and coffee. A maze of narrow streets and cobbled alleys rises away from the shore; seek out the car-free back lanes, where in places the 'paving' is simply the exposed bedrock. The area has more than 30 individual shops, galleries and privately run mini-museums, centred on the two streets of Välikatu and Itäinen Pitkäkatu.

Porvoon tuomiokirko (Porvoo Cathedral)

Rising above everything is the cathedral, a simple structure with ornate brick decoration on the gable-ends, and a separate bell-tower. The first church was established in the late 13th or early 14th century and extended in the 15th, giving it more or less its present shape, though it has been attacked and burned several times in its history. It became a cathedral in 1723, and here, at the Diet of Porvoo in 1809, the Finns gained the right to follow their own faith.

An arson attack in 2006 badly damaged the interior and necessitated extensive repairs. The first services were held at Advent 2008 and the cathedral reopened in 2009.

Porvoon tuomiokirko. Tel: (019) 6611 250. Open: May–Sept Mon–Fri 10am–6pm, Sat 10am–2pm, Sun 2–5pm; Oct–Apr Tue–Sat 10am–2pm, Sun 2–4pm.

TURKU (SWEDISH: ÅBO)

Founded in 1229, Turku is Finland's first city and first capital. Its great attractions are the cathedral and castle, separated by a 2km (1¼-mile) stretch of the River Aura. Five bridges span the river and a free and much-loved little ferry (*föri*) shuttles to and fro all day long. Other attractions lie on or close to the river and there are many floating restaurants.

Forum Marinum

Turku's maritime museum covers the entire history of seafaring, emphasising the local region. Moored alongside are several ships including the beautiful full-rigger *Suomen Joutsen* and the barque *Sigyn*, described as 'the last wooden three-masted sail-powered trading vessel in the world'.

Linnankatu 72. Tel: (02) 267 9511. www.forum-marinum.fi. Open: May–Sept daily 11am–7pm; Oct–Apr Tue–Sun 11am–6pm (museum ships May–Sept only). Admission charge.

Tuomiokirkko (Cathedral)

The national Mother Church, the cathedral was consecrated in 1300. The main external walls date from the late 15th and early 16th centuries. The interior was heavily restored after Turku's Great Fire in 1827. The 101m (331ft) tower, built after the fire, is a major landmark on the skyline.
*Tuomiokirkkonkatu 20.
Tel: (02) 261 7100. www.turunsrk.fi.
A museum in the south gallery is open daily except during services and church events. Admission charge.
Cathedral open: 9am–7pm (8pm in*

The view upriver at Turku

Ships moored at the Forum Marinum

summer), *except during services and church events.*

Turun linna (Turku Castle)

Finland's greatest castle embodies the city's primacy. Founded around 1280, the original citadel formed the basis of the main keep, with many additions over the centuries. Shifting political patterns and the development of powerful artillery diminished its military significance, but its solid granite construction made it too much trouble to demolish. Today, it houses a major historical museum.

Linnankatu 80. Tel: (02) 262 0300. www.nba.fi. Open: May–mid-Sept Tue–Sun 10am–6pm; mid-Sept–Apr Tue & Thur–Sun 10am–6pm, Wed noon–8pm. Admission charge.

NAANTALI

Naantali is a pretty and historic (founded 1443) seaside town 17km (11 miles) from Turku, with many well-preserved wooden houses and numerous galleries and craft shops. The view across the harbour is still dominated by the beautiful **Convent Church**. The nave dates from the mid-15th century, while the Baroque belfry was added in 1797.

Convent Church. Tel: (02) 437 5420. www.naantalinmatkailu.fi. Open: May daily 10am–6pm; Jun–Aug daily 10am–8pm; Sept–Apr Sun 11am–3pm, Wed noon–2pm. Free admission.

TURUN SAARISTO (THE TURKU ARCHIPELAGO)

The Turku Archipelago (Finnish: Turun Saaristo; Swedish: Åbo Skargård), variously credited with anything from 20,000 to 40,000 islands, is a region of tranquil beauty, best explored at a leisurely pace. A ring of larger islands is obvious on the map and is linked by bridges and ferries, a circuit of around 200km (125 miles). Further south, thousands of islands comprise the Archipelago National Park.

The archipelago merges with the Åland Islands (*see pp56–7*); the brighter red rock of Åland is the most obvious mark of the transition. Together they form the greatest, and for many the loveliest, archipelago in the world, traversed regularly by ferries between Turku and Mariehamn.

THE ÅLAND ISLANDS

The Åland archipelago links Finland and Sweden, physically and culturally. Incorporated into Finland in 1809, the 'Åland question' remained a vexed issue until 1921, when the League of Nations confirmed Finnish sovereignty, albeit with considerable autonomy. The islands are Swedish-speaking, with their own flag, their own stamps and a Parliament with tax-raising powers.

The archipelago numbers around 6,500 islands, the main one being by far the largest island in Finland. Rocky shores of reddish granite fringe landscapes noted for their spring flowers, rich farmland and woodland. The principal islands are linked by bridges, causeways and local ferries, some of which carry only bikes and pedestrians.

The approach to Mariehamn passes the old pilot station of Kobba Klintar, sturdily planted on an islet; used until 1972, it's now a popular destination for boat trips, with a summer café.

Mariehamn

Mariehamn, with its tree-lined streets, occupies an isthmus between harbours. The western, **Västra Hamnen**, is where ferries and cruise ships dock, but the town centre is closer to **Östra Hamnen**. It's easy to get around on foot, and a free bus service tours the town every half hour. Mariehamn has a strong seafaring tradition and fostered many prosperous shipowners.

Pommern at Mariehamn

Pommern

Pommern is one of the last great sailing ships. A 4-masted steel-hulled barque, built at Glasgow in 1903, she grosses 2,376 tons and is 95m (312ft) long. The main mast is 50m (165ft) high and the total sail area over 3,000sq m (32,300sq ft). Steam was used for loading and for raising the anchor, not for propulsion. *Västra Hamnen. Tel: (018) 531 421. www.mariehamn.ax. Open: May, Jun & Aug daily 9am–5pm; Jul daily 9am–7pm; Sept daily 10am–4pm. Admission charge.*

Sjökvarteret (Maritime Quarter)

This intriguing area includes an active boatyard, smithy and other craft workshops. Several ships built here are based at the quay and day cruises are sometimes available.

North end of Östra Hamnen: open daily.
Museum of Shipbuilding. Tel: (018) 160
33. www.visitaland.com. Open: mid-
Jun–mid-Aug daily 10am–6pm; mid-
Aug–mid-Jun Mon–Fri 9am–11am.
Admission charge.

Away from Mariehamn

The district of Sund, in the northeast of
the main island, has several attractions.

Bomarsund Fortress

The fortress was built by the Russians,
beginning in 1832 and never finished.
Its mighty ramparts give some of the
best views over the archipelago. The site
is open and free to visit.

Jan Karlsgården

An open-air museum recreating a
typical Åland farm of the 19th century.
Tel: (018) 432 134. Open: May–
mid-Sept 10am–5pm. Free admission.

TALL SHIPS

Many magnificent sailing ships are berthed in
Baltic ports. These include:
– *Götheborg*, a replica of an 18th-century East
Indiaman, based in Göteborg.
– *Dar Pomorza*, a frigate from 1909, based in
Gdynia.
– *Suomen Joutsen*, a full-rigger built in 1902,
now at Forum Marinum in Turku.
– *af Chapman*, a steel full-rigged ship built
1888, moored in Stockholm, Sweden, and
used as a hostel.
– *Pommern*, built 1903, moored at
Mariehamn.
– *Passat*, built 1911, moored at Travemünde.
The famous Tall Ships' Races regularly visit
the Baltic: it last did so in 2009 and is next
due in 2013.

Kastelholms Slot

A fine medieval castle, now restored.
Tel: (018) 432 150. Open: May &
Sept 10am–4pm; Jun & Aug
10am–5pm; Jul 10am–6pm.
Admission charge.

Finland

Kobba Klintar on the approach to Mariehamn

Russia

Russia is vast, the world's largest country, spanning 11 time zones and stretching from the easternmost point of Asia to the borders of the European Union. In earlier times, both under the tsars and in the Soviet era, its power extended even further, and its influence is felt in many of the other countries around the Baltic, especially Finland, the Baltic States and Poland.

ST PETERSBURG

Founded in 1703 as Russia's 'Window on the West', St Petersburg has packed plenty of history into its 300-odd years, and was Russia's capital for most of them. Above all, it was the centre of the world-changing revolution of 1917, yet the city that the visitor sees is overwhelmingly of the preceding centuries, extravagantly endowed with palaces, cathedrals, bridges (more than 300 of them) and other great monuments from this period.

Many of these are on the grand scale, as is the city itself. It's by far the largest city on the Baltic, with over 5 million people – nearly three times the size of the next largest, Stockholm. Between the Winter Palace and the Petropavlovskaya Fortress, the river Neva is around 500m (1,640ft) wide, more than twice as wide as the Thames in London.

The scale of the city means that it's not practical to see it all on foot (even discounting the out-of-city attractions like Peterhof and Pushkin). Walking everywhere would mean many hours pounding the city's unyielding (and in places notoriously uneven) pavements. Fortunately, there's abundant, and cheap, public transport, including the world's deepest metro.

Founded on the marshy delta of the Neva, St Petersburg sprawls over several islands as well as the mainland on both

Isaakievskiy sobor

sides (the northern side is often called the Petrograd side). The central district, south of the river, is laced with rivers and canals, created to control flooding; water tours are very popular and an excellent way to see the area.

Today, St Petersburg is once again the Window on the West; home to many Western companies, banks and consulates, it has become a cosmopolitan modern metropolis. Visitors will never forget that they are

in Russia, however, and it will strike the majority as the most exotic destination on the Baltic, as well as the grandest.

Approaches
It must be said that the approach to St Petersburg is not as inspiring as, say, that to Helsinki or Oslo. There may be glimpses of the great palace and park of Peterhof (*see p72*), and there will certainly be a chance to look at the fortress island of Kronstadt, but as the

(*Cont. on p62*)

St Petersburg

Russia's Revolutions

We may speak of 'the Russian Revolution', but really there were three. Their root causes included the immense disparities between the wealthy and powerful and the lower classes; the great palaces of St Petersburg testify eloquently to one side of this divide. Industrialisation and mass communication brought this inequality into sharper focus. The assassination of the reforming tsar, Alexander II, in 1881 also opened a new era of repression, exacerbating tensions.

The 1905 Revolution
The Russo-Japanese War and an economic slump fuelled discontent. Strikes and demonstrations were met with violence, deepening the unrest. Finally the hierarchy made some grudging concessions, including the establishment of a Parliament, the Duma, though it had little real power. The lid was – temporarily – back on the pot.

1917 – The February Revolution
World War I intensified social problems and unrest. This found its focus in Petrograd (as St Petersburg was then known). Strikes and demonstrations arose spontaneously. With troops at the front, the army could not suppress the risings, and Tsar Nicholas II abdicated. Members of the Duma then established a provisional government, based in the Winter Palace.

However, the provisional government never enjoyed clear popular support, and was challenged by the Petrograd Soviet, which represented workers and soldiers. Meanwhile, the militant socialist

Smolny Institute

Aurora fired the first shot in the October Revolution

Vladimir Ilyich Lenin returned to Petrograd in order to galvanise the Bolsheviks. Attempts by both the Bolsheviks and the army to seize power were abortive, however.

1917 – The October Revolution

While the previous uprisings had arisen spontaneously, October's was carefully planned by Lenin (*see p63*) and the Bolsheviks. Its central event was an assault on the Winter Palace, planned and led by Leon Trotsky, creator of the Red Army. While the Bolsheviks took control of Petrograd and Moscow, resistance elsewhere was widespread, from other parties of the Left as well as from the Right.

The Bolshevik leadership left Petrograd for Moscow in March 1918. A bloody civil war dragged on until 1923, its protagonists being labelled Reds (the Bolsheviks and their allies) and Whites (a coalition of monarchists, nationalists and others, supported by many Western powers).

Revolutionary sites
Palace Square and the Winter Palace
(*see pp62 & 70*)

The focal point of many demonstrations. The taking of the Winter Palace was the decisive moment of the October Revolution.

Smolny Institute

Headquarters of the Bolshevik Government after the October Revolution: Lenin lived and worked here for 124 days. *Not open to public. Nearest metro: Chernyshevskaya (continue west to Tavricheskiy dvorets).*

Tavricheskiy dvorets (Tauride Palace)

Base of the Petrograd Soviet before the October Revolution. *Not open to the public. Nearest metro: Chernyshevskaya.*

Gulf of Finland funnels into the Neva River, the scale of the city is evident mostly in its vast dockyards and massive housing projects, Soviet-era and contemporary. In the final stages the graceful face of the city becomes apparent. Cruise ships moor on the banks of the Bolshaya (Greater) Neva just below Most Leytenanta Shmidta (Lieutenant Schmidt Bridge). Several key sights (notably St Isaac's Cathedral) are within reasonable walking distance, and the St Petersburg walk (*see pp66–7*) starts here. The nearest metro station is Vasileostrovskaya, about a ten-minute walk from the bridge: take the street running away from the river, just downstream from the bridge (6–7 linii); for much of its length it's pleasantly pedestrianised.

The Bronze Horseman honours Peter the Great

South of the Neva
Bronze Horseman

To the north of St Isaac's Cathedral, this statue is a monument to the city's founder, Peter the Great, established by order of the other 'Great' tsar, Catherine II. Designed by Etienne Falconet, the statue was unveiled in 1782, and yet it looks strangely modern, especially the wave-like forms of its granite plinth.
Ploshchad Dekabristov.

Dvortsovaya ploshchad (Palace Square)

Dvortsovaya ploshchad is set between the great Winter Palace and the even longer frontage of the General Staff building. It was planned (by Carlo Rossi) to accommodate large-scale military parades and drills, and of course saw huge gatherings during the revolutionary ferment of 1917. Today, it is occasionally used for open-air concerts. Its focus is the 47m (154ft) Alexander Column, erected in 1834 to commemorate the 1812 victory over Napoleon. The shaft is a single block of red granite, simply resting on its plinth and secured solely by its own weight. For more on the Winter Palace, see the feature on **The Hermitage** (*pp70–71*).

Isaakievskiy sobor (St Isaac's Cathedral)

The gilded dome of St Isaac's, rising over 100m (328ft), remains a prime landmark of St Petersburg, whose central district has no high-rise

buildings. The present cathedral is the fourth to stand here and was built between 1818 and 1858 to plans by Auguste de Montferrand. The exterior is faced in grey marble, with columns of red granite; the interior is more lavish, with multicoloured marble, semi-precious stones and over 60 mosaics. It can accommodate around 14,000 worshippers, who stand, as is traditional in Orthodox churches. Closed during Stalin's time, it later reopened as a museum; it now stages services on the main holy days. Visitors may also climb to the colonnade supporting the main dome, for a grand view over the city.
Isaakievskaya ploshchad 1.
Tel: (812) 315 9732. Open: Thur–Tue 11am–7pm (last entry 6pm, colonnade 1hr earlier). Admission charge. Note: buy tickets inside the entrance, not at the booth outside (this is for Russians only).

Kazanskiy sobor (Kazan Cathedral)

From Nevskiy prospekt, Kazan Cathedral is fronted by a huge semi-circular colonnade of 96 columns. Built between 1801 and 1811, its pioneering iron dome rises more than 70m (230ft) above the ground. For the devout, however, its significance is as the home of the icon of Our Lady of Kazan, credited with several miracles. On entering, it's clear that this is no museum but a living place of worship (though visitors are welcome). The interior, with its massive granite columns, is dark and atmospheric, lit by innumerable candles. In one

LENIN

Vladimir Ilyich Ulyanov was born in 1870. As a student he became radicalised, influenced by the execution of his elder brother. Expelled from university, he moved to St Petersburg and dedicated himself to revolutionary politics, taking the pseudonym Lenin. After exile in Siberia, he spent most of the following years in Western Europe, returning after the first 1917 Revolution before being forced to seek refuge in Finland for three months.

In October 1917, Lenin returned to St Petersburg to lead the second Revolution, becoming head of government and carrying out major economic reforms. His health was damaged by an assassination attempt in 1918, which also weakened his hold on power. He died in 1924, opening the way for the calamitous reign of Stalin.

corner a priest chants resonantly. One cannot fail to observe – respectfully – frequent acts of devotion, from the kissing of icons to occasional prostration. It's thought-provoking that most of these worshippers must have been born and raised under a militantly anti-religious regime.
Kazanskaya ploshchad 2.
Tel: (812) 318 4528. Open: daily 9am–6pm. Free admission.

Khram Spas-na-Krovi (Church of the Saviour on the Spilled Blood)

Officially called the Church of the Resurrection, this is for many visitors the most 'Russian' church in St Petersburg, spectacularly ornamented in multicoloured brick, mosaic and tile. It was erected, as a memorial, on the

Russia

site where Tsar Alexander II received mortal wounds in 1881, and completed in 1907. Belying the recent date, the style is consciously old-fashioned. The interior is – if possible – even more breathtaking. Great mosaics cover the walls, portraying biblical scenes. The magnificent floor uses many varieties of Italian marble.

Nab. Kanala Griboyebedova 2a.
Tel: (812) 315 1636. Open: Thur–Tue 11am–6pm. Admission charge. Note: buy tickets inside the entrance, not at the booth outside (this is for Russians only).

The colourful exterior of the Khram Spas-na-Krovi

Letniy Sad (Summer Garden) and Letniy dvorets (Summer Palace)

Letniy Sad is St Petersburg's oldest garden, created in 1704. Peter the Great, a 'hands-on' ruler, was personally involved in its planning. With its many mature trees, the garden has lost some of its original formality, and feels pleasantly detached from the roar of traffic. Its paths are lined with sculptures, mostly by Italian artists of the 17th and 18th centuries, with a few engaging newer pieces – look out for the giant chairs.

At the northeast corner of the gardens, Letniy Dvorets is a modest establishment (by St Petersburg standards, anyway). It was built in 1710–12 to plans by Domenico Trezzini, and has just seven rooms on each of its two floors, all of them restored to look as they did when they were occupied by Tsar Peter and his family.

Dvorets Petra 1. Tel: (812) 314 0456.
Gardens open: May–Sept 10am–10pm; Oct–Mar 10am–6pm.
Palace open: May–Oct Wed–Sun 10am–6pm, Mon 10am–5pm.
Admission charge.

Nevskiy prospekt

Nevskiy prospekt is the main axis of central St Petersburg. It stretches approximately 4.5km (2¾ miles), from close by Dvortsovaya ploshchad to the Alexander Nevskiy Monastery, with just one slight change of alignment near the Moscow Station. It crosses three bridges

Letniy Sad, a peaceful oasis in the middle of the city

and is served by three metro stations. Naturally it plays host to many of the city's leading shops, restaurants and cafés as well.

Russkiy Muzyei (Russian Museum)
The State Russian Museum hosts the world's largest collection of Russian art, complementing the 'foreign' collections of the Hermitage. Established in 1898, it now occupies four separate buildings, but the main collection is housed in the **Mikhailovskiy Palace**, around the corner from the Church of the Saviour on the Spilled Blood. Here is the broad sweep of Russian art – painting, sculpture, applied and decorative arts – from the 14th century to the early 20th. The building itself dates from 1819 and is by Carlo Rossi. More recent Russian art is shown at the museum's branch in the **Marble Palace**.
Mikhailovskiy Palace, ploshchad Isskustv. Tel: (812) 595 4248.

www.rusmuseum.ru.
Open: Wed–Sun 10am–5pm, Mon 10am–4pm. Admission charge.
Marble Palace, Milionnaya ulitsa 5/1. Tel: (812) 312 9054. Open: hours as above. Admission charge.

Statue of Catherine the Great
Catherine the Great, who reigned for 34 years (1762–96), is commemorated in a small garden just off Nevskiy prospekt. Catherine was German by birth, succeeding to the throne after a coup d'état deposed her ineffectual husband, Peter III. The monument, unveiled in 1873, was designed by Mikhail Mikeshin and incorporates the efforts of three other sculptors. Around the base are leading figures of the age: the lone woman is Yekaterina Dashkova, who rose to chair the Russian Academy of Sciences.
Ploshchad Ostrovskovo.

Walk: St Petersburg

The walk covers most of the central sights, and also links several of St Petersburg's most important parks and gardens.

Start at most Leytenanta Shmidta, the first bridge upstream from the cruise quays. If you're not already on the mainland side, cross the bridge to get there. Follow the embankment upstream to an open space on the right, Ploshchad Dekabristov.

Walk through the gardens, passing the statue of the **Bronze Horseman** (*see p62*), towards **St Isaac's Cathedral** (*see p62*): if you want to visit now, the entrance is at the far side. Otherwise turn left before reaching it, to walk through the Aleksandrovskiy Gardens, with the massive Admiralty building on the left.

At the end, cross the road into **Dvortsovaya ploshchad** (Palace Square; *see p62*); the Winter Palace is on the left, the General Staff building to the right. Leave the square, keeping the latter close on your right, and quickly come to the Pevcheskiy most (Pevcheskiy Bridge). This forms a sort of small square. Opposite this is a courtyard with iron gates. Enter,

then go through the archway in the far right corner to walk through a series of typical St Petersburg yards. The communicating arches are almost, but not quite, in line.

Emerge into a street and turn left, then right at the top, and you're soon confronted by the **Church of the Saviour on the Spilled Blood** (*see pp63–4*). Continue past it to enter the Mikhailovsky Gardens. Wander through these, exit and turn left to cross a bridge over the Moyka River. Cross the road ahead, to the corner of Marsovo Pole (The Field of Mars), then turn immediately right across another busy road. Continue ahead to an entrance into **Letniy Sad** (the Summer Garden; *see p64*).

Skirt a pond then follow the central path. Approaching the far end, turn right to visit **Letniy dvorets** (the Summer Palace; *see p64*); otherwise exit the park and turn left along the Neva embankment.

Cross Troitskiy most (Trinity Bridge) to the Petrograd side and turn right along the Petrovskaya embankment. Pass **Domik Petra** (Peter the Great's log cabin; *see pp68–9*) and continue to the cruiser *Aurora* (*see p68*).

Backtrack from here almost to Troitskiy most, then turn right through Troitskaya ploshchad, aiming for the far left corner. Cross an intersection to reach the narrow bridge (Ioannovskiy most), which leads to the **Petropavlovskaya krepost** (Peter and Paul Fortress; *see p69*). Follow the main spine route to the square in front of the **Cathedral** (*see p69*), then turn right. As you exit the gate, look to the right to see Kronverk (the Artillery Museum).

Turn left, cross another bridge and then turn left along the embankment. Cross the next bridge, Birzhevoy most, onto **Vasilevskiy Island** (*see p68*). Pass the first of the great **Rostral Columns** (*see p68*), then follow the bulge of the Spit around to the second column. Cross the road then follow Universitetskaya embankment. Pass the end of the 400m (1,312ft) long main building of St Petersburg University (masked by trees, its length is hard to appreciate) and the yellow **Menshikov Palace,** a branch of the **Hermitage** (*see pp70–71*). Further along the embankment, opposite the Academy of Arts, are two granite sphinxes, brought from Egypt in 1832. Just beyond is most Leytenanta Shmidta and the completion of the circuit.

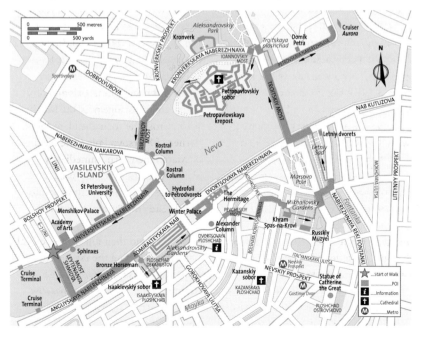

The Rostral Columns and the Old Stock Exchange on Vasilevskiy Island

Vasilevskiy Island

Vasilevskiy Island has a plethora of museums and palaces, but the key reason to go there is to visit its easternmost point, known as the **Spit**, for its awe-inspiring view of the river and the city – one of the world's grandest city views.

A massive new array of fountains plays just offshore on certain days and even 'dances' to music on special occasions (enquire at tourist information points for schedules).

Flanking the Spit are two **Rostral Columns**, erected in 1810. They originally served as lighthouses when the area was an active port, and still bear lights on festival days. The design, adorned with metal ships' prows (Latin: *rostra*), follows ancient Roman tradition.

North of the Neva
Cruiser *Aurora*

The *Aurora* is famous for firing the shot that launched the October Revolution (ironically, perhaps, it was a blank round). Launched in 1900, *Aurora* saw action in the Russo-Japanese War of 1904–5. She's now restored and serves as a museum and also as a training ship.
Petrovskaya naberezhnaya. www.aurora.org.ru. Open: Wed–Sun 10.30am–4.30pm (closed last Wed of month). Free admission.

Domik Petra
(Peter the Great's log cabin)

Peter the Great had this simple dwelling built as his first residence in the new city. It has just two main rooms, a study and a dining room, where he also slept.

Russia

CRIME AND PUNISHMENT

St Petersburg is a key setting for two of the greatest novels of all time, Tolstoy's *Anna Karenina* and Dostoyevsky's *Crime and Punishment*. Dostoyevsky spent much of his life in St Petersburg and the city may almost be seen as a character in the novel. Its main protagonist, Raskolnikov, commits murder, which he initially justifies to himself on rational grounds. Increasingly tormented by guilt and paranoia, it's only when he confesses and is sent to a penal camp in Siberia that he finds some sense of his own humanity and discovers the ability to love another.

Today, rather oddly, it's been enveloped by a brick construction, but the interior is little changed.

Petrovskaya naberezhnaya 6.
Tel: (812) 314 0574. www.rusmuseum.
ru/eng. Open: Wed–Sun 10am–6pm,
Mon 10am–5pm. Admission charge.
Metro: Krestovskiy Ostrov.

Petropavlovskaya krepost (Peter and Paul Fortress)

Having wrested control of the area from the Swedes in 1703, Peter the Great set out to protect Russian access to the Baltic, and began by establishing a fortress on the island of Zayachiy Ostrov. Simple defences were finished that same summer. Then began the longer task of creating great stone ramparts, entrusted to one of 'Peter's Italians', Domenico Trezzini. During the day you may wander freely through the precincts of the fortress, and its river frontage is a popular bathing spot in the summer. Within the area are several museums and, of prime interest, the city's first cathedral.

Zayachiy Ostrov. Open: Thur–Tue
10am–6pm. Admission charge.
Metro: Gorkovskaya.

Petropavlovskiy sobor (Peter and Paul Cathedral)

Perhaps Trezzini's masterpiece, built 1712–33, the cathedral would not look out of place in Turin or Milan. Its slender, gilded spire is topped by a flying angel. The interior has one dominating – and wholly Russian – feature: the great iconostasis, carved in wood to the designs of Ivan Zarudzny. From its foundation until the 1917 Revolutions, the cathedral was the burial place of the tsars and their immediate family; in 1998 the last tsar, Nicholas II, was reinterred here with state honours.

Open: Thur–Tue 10am–6pm.

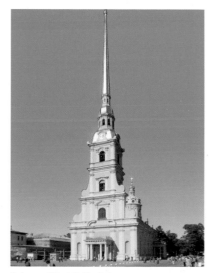

Peter and Paul Cathedral

The Hermitage

Like much in St Petersburg, the Hermitage is on a grand scale. The Winter Palace, vast in itself, is less than half of the whole, which includes four linked buildings, plus several other sites around the city. Its importance is twofold. First, it preserves the grand rooms of the Winter Palace as they were when it was the main residence of the tsars. The second is as one of the world's leading art museums, holding over three million items.

The Winter Palace

The Winter Palace is the architectural jewel in the Hermitage crown. It was built between 1754 and 1762 to the designs of Italian Bartolomeo Francesco Rastrelli. A major fire in 1837 destroyed most of the interior; reconstruction was relatively swift and the opportunity was taken to remodel many of the great rooms, giving them largely the forms we see today. The Winter Palace was also at the centre of events during Russia's Revolutions (*see pp60–61*).

The palace makes an immediate impact (immediate, that is, once you've queued to get in) with the Main, or Jordan, Staircase. Other rooms that were designed to impress, and generally succeed, include the Armorial Hall and St George's Hall (the Large Throne Room).

Other buildings

Four further buildings were progressively added to the Hermitage complex, all connected by enclosed bridges. These have their own grand rooms, such as the Italian Skylight Hall in the New Hermitage, with its huge malachite vases. A favourite with many is the frothy Pavilion Hall in the Small Hermitage ('small' is relative!).

Hermitage collections

It should be noted that the Hermitage collections do not include much Russian art – the Russian Museum is the place for seeing that. Apart from a suite of Romanov portraits, some of them larger than life, the Hermitage collection is mainly devoted to European art, from antiquity to the early 20th century (no prizes for guessing why acquisitions ceased after 1917). Pride of place probably goes to the Renaissance masters, including two paintings by Leonardo da Vinci (no more than 15 survive in the entire world). There are also tremendous assemblages of French, German and Flemish art. Among the

The Winter Palace is just as it was when the tsars lived there

Dutch masters, the Hermitage has more than 20 Rembrandts.

Visiting the Hermitage

It's impossible to see everything in a day, and exhausting even to attempt it. A sensible plan would be to take in the main state rooms of the Winter Palace, where you first arrive, and then to select elements of the collection according to your particular interest or inclination.

The Hermitage gets extremely busy. You'll usually have to queue to get in; at peak periods this could take an hour, shuffling slowly through the courtyard of the Winter Palace. It seems to be perfectly acceptable for groups to take it in turns to hold the place in the queue while others visit the small café in the courtyard.

Visiting with a prebooked group, an option most cruises will offer, will spare you most of the waiting, but loses you the chance to explore the Hermitage in your own time.

Entrance on Palace Square.
Tel: (812) 710 9079.
www.hermitagemuseum.org.
Open: Tue–Sat 10.30am–6pm, Sun 10.30am–5pm. Admission charge.
Metro: Nevskiy Prospekt.

The Grand Cascade leads the eye up to the Grand Palace at Peterhof

AROUND ST PETERSBURG
Petrodvorets (Peterhof)

Petrodvorets lies 30km (19 miles) west of the city, on the shores of the Gulf of Finland. Dubbed the 'Russian Versailles', Peterhof was the first imperial palace to be built outside St Petersburg. The quickest way there is by hydrofoil from the Neva embankment. It's much cheaper, however, to take a train from the Baltiskaya Station to Novyy Petergof. Frequent buses make the connection from there – all seem to display the word 'Fountains'. Alternatively it's a walk of about 2km (1¼ miles): follow ulitsa Aurora then turn left on Sankt-Peterburgskiy prospekt. Both the park and the palace complex include a number of specialist museums.

The Lower Park

Arrive by sea, and it's the Lower Park you'll see first, with its central avenue leading the eye to the Bolshoy dvorets (Grand Palace). The park encompasses formal gardens and more natural-looking areas – the shoreline is popular for picnics. It includes the palace of **Monplaisir**, the first to be built here, and several other smaller palaces and villas. There's even one called the **Cottage Palace** – surely a contradiction in terms. However, what makes the greatest impression is the profusion of fountains – more than 120 in all, plus several cascades, and all fed by gravity, without a single pump. At the focal point below the Grand Palace is Carlo Bartolomeo Rastrelli's gilded *Samson Rending Open the Jaws of the Lion*, surrounded by lesser fountains and flanked by cascades: quite a spectacle. *Lower Park. Tel: (812) 420 0073. Open: daily 9am–8pm. Free admission. Fountains operate late May–early Oct Mon–Fri 11am–6pm, Sat & Sun 11am–7pm.*

Bolshoy dvorets (The Grand Palace)

Formerly the main summer residence of the tsars, the Grand Palace was built in 1714–25, and subsequently extended and remodelled by Francesco Bartolomeo Rastrelli. Its façades are among the most elegant of all the great palaces. Some rooms retain the original Baroque décor, while others were later redesigned. It suffered severe damage during World War II, when it fell into German hands, and some restoration work remains to be completed.

http://peterhofmuseum.ru. Open: Tue–Sun 10.30am–5.30pm (closed last Tue in the month). Admission charge.

Pushkin and Pavlovsk

South of the city, Pushkin and Pavlovsk are served by trains from the Vitebsk station: the stop for Pushkin is called Detskoe Selo. Use local buses to join the dots (it would be a long walk!).

Pushkin (Tsarskoye Selo)

Formerly called Tsarskoye Selo, Pushkin boasts two palaces with their attendant parks and lesser buildings. Its centrepiece, the **Catherine Palace**, dates from the late 18th century and was begun by the Scottish architect Charles Cameron. Its highly ornamental façades are outshone by the barely believable Amber Room. Its decorations were stolen by Nazi forces, but re-created from photographs and records and reinaugurated in 2003, St Petersburg's tercentenary.

Pushkin. Tel: (812) 466 6669.
Open: Wed–Mon 10am–5pm (closed last Mon in the month). Admission charge.

Pavlovsk

Pavlovsk offers interesting contrasts with Pushkin, and indeed with most of the other great palaces. The park is laid out in an 'English' style (think Capability Brown), while the palace, by Charles Cameron, has three main blocks linked by curved wings around an elliptical courtyard.

Pavlovsk. Tel: (812) 470 2156.
Open: Sat–Thur 10am–5pm (closed first Mon in the month). Admission charge.

Beautiful gilding on the exterior of the Grand Palace, Peterhof

The Baltic republics

Estonia, Latvia and Lithuania are often lumped together, and they do have much in common, including parallel tracks of recent history: independence in 1918 after centuries of foreign domination; annexation by the Soviets in 1940; a few years of German occupation; the return of Soviet rule until 1991.

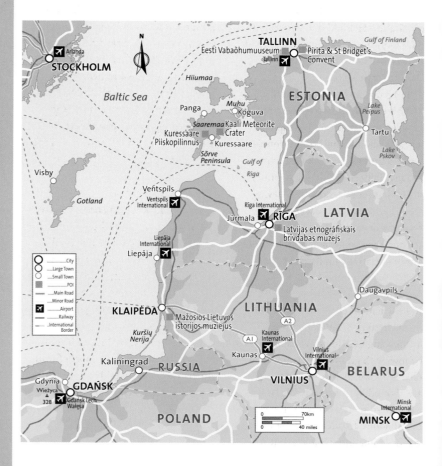

Today, all three are EU members and making rapid strides, without losing touch with their past. It would, however, be a mistake to think of them as all the same. Each has a strong sense of nationhood and a distinct culture, and Estonia is further distinguished by its language, akin to Finnish and totally different from the Slavic tongues of Latvia and Lithuania.

ESTONIA

Estonia's closeness to Finland, both physically – Helsinki is a mere 80km (50 miles) from Tallinn – and culturally, has given it something of a head start since independence, as the swagger of Tallinn's downtown skyline testifies. So far, this economic development has been heavily concentrated in the capital, home to about a third of the population but accounting for half of economic activity. Tallinn is also overwhelmingly the main tourist destination, leaving the rest of Estonia – peaceful countryside, vast forests, a lovely coastline and some delightful historic towns – relatively undiscovered.

Tallinn

If anywhere deserves the epithet 'city of contrasts', it's Tallinn, with its astonishing Old Town, Vanalinn, cheek by jowl with gleaming new tower blocks. However, by ordinance, none are allowed to overtop St Olav's Church, so the Old Town can never be overshadowed. Indeed, for many visitors, Vanalinn *is* Tallinn, but that's

regrettable; there's much more to discover, whether it's bargain-hunting in the new city, the attractions of Kadriorg (more contrasts!), or the breezy shorelines beyond. Incidentally, Reval – a name that crops up everywhere – is simply the old name for Tallinn.

Approaches

Cruise ships dock at the north side of the harbour; the scheduled ferries (Tallink *et al.*) berth even closer to the city. The cruise terminal is about ten minutes' walk from Vanalinn, and if no shuttle bus is available, you'll have to walk, as you'll first meet city transport at the edge of Vanalinn. Exit the cruise terminal and turn right along the first street, Sadama. Carry on to a large intersection. As you pass a petrol station, cross the road and tram tracks, then bear right.

Vanalinn (Old Town)

Tallinn's Old Town has few rivals, and surely no betters, anywhere in Europe. To find such a complete medieval townscape anywhere is remarkable; to find it in a capital city, and one that has changed hands several times, is nothing short of astounding. And yet, though it beggars belief, the Communist Government in the 1960s seriously considered demolishing most of it in the name of 'progress'. Now Vanalinn, in its entirety, is a World Heritage Site.

Vanalinn is a labyrinth of narrow streets spiralling to the commanding

(*Cont. on p78*)

Walk: Tallinn

This is essentially a Vanalinn tour; its convolutions exemplify the labyrinthine nature of the place. The distance is short, but if you stop at even half of the places of interest along the way it could occupy a full, and very rewarding, day.

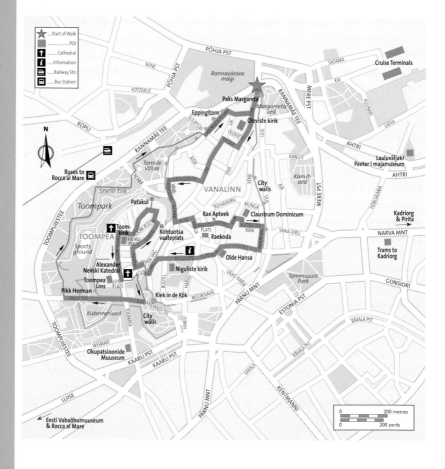

Start at the northern gate of **Vanalinn** (*see p75*), where you naturally arrive if you've walked from the harbour. The big tower on the left is Paks Margareta (Fat Margaret). Go straight up the street (Pikk). Turn right on Pagari, under a bridge. You're now passing the former KGB HQ; bricked-up cellar windows hint at its sinister history.

Turn left on Lai (detour right to visit **Oleviste kirik**; *see p78*), then third right on Suur-Kloostri to reach another gate and a well-preserved section of the walls. A small door just left of the gateway gives access to the wall and three towers.

Continue, inside the walls, on Väike-Kloostri. Bear left on a wider street (Nunne), then second left (Pikk again). Turn right on Kinga, which leads to **Raekoja plats** (*see p79*) at the heart of Vanalinn. Turn left, go past **Rae Apteek** (*see pp78–9*) and down Apteegi. Turn left, then shortly right under an arch into Katariina käik (or go a bit further along the street first to find the **Dominican Cloister**; *see p78*).

Turn right, walking below the city walls to Viru. Turn left briefly to see the gate, then backtrack and continue up Viru. Bear left (passing Olde Hansa) and continue up Kuninga and Niguliste, passing the tourist information centre. On the left is **Niguliste kirik** (*see p78*).

Continue up the steps of Lühike jaig, then go right, through an archway under a tower to reach **Toompea** (*see p79*). Bear left up Pikk jaig,

glimpsing **Alexander Nevski Katedral** (*see pp79–80*) ahead. Turn right on Piiskopi, then bear right at Kiriku plats into Kohtu. Soon there's a platform on the right, with views over Vanalinn and downtown. Leaving here, go straight ahead then right on Tööm-Rüütli; follow it round then go right under an arch to another viewpoint (Patakul).

Return through the arch, go straight ahead to return to Kiriku plats and turn right. At the far corner of the square, Toom-Kooli goes two ways: take the left branch to Lossi plats, between **Toompea Loss** (*see pp80–81*) and Alexander Nevski Katedral. Beyond Toompea Loss is Kuberneriaed (the Governor's Garden).

Pass the right side of Alexander Nevski Katedral, then go right down steps to **Kiek in de Kök** (*see p80*). Just below is a street, Komandandi tee. Turn right up here and go straight on to descend Falgi tee. Bear right on a path below the tall tower, Pikk Herman, descend steps, go through a car park and skirt a sports ground to reach the green Toompark.

Follow a path alongside a small lake (a remnant of moat). At its end, cross a street and continue into the gardens of Tornide Väljak (Towers Square), with good views of a string of towers. At the far end, go through the breach in the wall, then turn immediately left on Laboratooriumi. This passes the Eppingitorn (Epping Tower) before it returns you to Pikk, close to the start of the tour.

heights of Toompea. It's simply made for wandering: quirky perspectives shift constantly; colourful façades catch the eye; tempting alleys and steps lead who knows where. If your feet get sore, there's always a handy bar or café just round the corner. Throughout Vanalinn, acrylic wall-plaques, in Estonian and English, give details of all the most interesting buildings.

City walls Originally, Vanalinn was encircled by 4km (2½ miles) of continuous wall, of which half remains. Several towers can be visited and on the west side of town you can explore a section of the wooden galleries, including three towers. Access to the walls is by a door just left of the gateway on Suur-Kloostri. The first spiral stairway will deter vertigo sufferers; while the stairs to the upper reaches of Nunnatorn are dark and precipitous (*see also Kiek in de Kök, p80*). *Gümnaasiumi 3. Tel: (372) 644 9867. Open: Jun–Aug daily 11am–7pm; Apr & May, Sept & Oct Mon–Wed & Fri noon–6pm, Sat & Sun 11am–4pm; Nov–Mar Mon–Tue & Fri noon–5pm, Sat & Sun 11am–4pm. Admission charge.*

Claustrum Dominicum (Dominican Cloister and Museum) Tallinn's oldest building is the surviving east wing of a Dominican monastery, with lovely cloisters, library, refectory and monks' dormitory. The **Dominnklaste Kloostri Muuseum** focuses on the rich tradition of stone-carving.

Cloister: Müürivahe 33. Tel: (372) 511 2536. Open: Jun–Aug daily 10.30am–5pm. Admission charge.
Museum: Vene 16. Tel: (372) 515 5489. www.kloostri.ee. Open: mid-May–Aug daily 10am–6pm. Admission charge.

Niguliste kirik (St Nicholas's Church) Another glorious medieval church, Niguliste is now a branch of the national Art Museum, dedicated to religious art. Its pride and joy is the 15th-century *Danse macabre* by Bernt Notke, actually one panel of a four-part work originating in Lübeck. *Niguliste 3. Tel: (02) 631 4330. www.ekm.ee. Open: Wed–Sun 10am–5pm. Admission charge.*

Oleviste kirik (St Olav's Church) Named for the Norwegian saint-king, the church dates from the 13th century. In 1509 its 159m (522ft) spire was the tallest manmade structure on Earth. Later alterations have reduced its height somewhat, but at 124m (407ft) it's still impressive and for those who make the climb there's an unrivalled view of Vanalinn. *Lai 50. Tel: (372) 641 2241. Open: Apr–Oct daily 10am–6pm. Admission charge.*

Rae Apteek (Town Pharmacy) Already in existence in 1422, this is the oldest continuously operating pharmacy in the world. Some modern refinements have been discreetly incorporated into the working area, while in a side room

Rooftops of Vanalinn with the tall spire of Oleviste kirik

there is a selection of old remedies and related paraphernalia on display. *Raekoja plats 11. Tel: (372) 631 4860. Open: Tue–Sat 10am–6pm. Free admission.*

Raekoda (Town Hall) Europe's best-preserved medieval Town Hall, Raekoda existed before 1322, but was substantially remodelled at the start of the 15th century. You can climb the tower (115 steps) for a great view. *Raekoja plats 1. Tel: (372) 645 7900. www.tallinn.ee. Open: Jul & Aug Mon–Sat 10am–4pm; May, Jun & Sept Tue–Sat 10am–4pm. Admission charge.*

Raekoja plats (Town Hall Square) A market- and meeting-place since time immemorial, this is the focal point of Vanalinn. Colourful façades line three

sides, while the fourth is filled by the limestone walls and slender tower of Raekoda itself. Unsurprisingly, most of the buildings around the square now house cafés and restaurants.

Toompea and around
Today, Toompea just feels like a higher part of Vanalinn; it's only from the west, in Toompark, that you get a real sense of its impressive natural crags and mighty walls. With two cathedrals, and the seat of government, it's worth separate consideration.

Alexander Nevski Katedral At Lossi plats, the sugary pink Toompea Loss confronts the even more elaborate confection of Alexander Nevski Katedral, which exemplifies the tsarist era. It's relatively new, completed in

The pink side of Toompea Loss

1900. The interior is richly ornamented with icons and mosaics. Services are held daily at 8.30am, before which the bells, the largest ensemble in Tallinn, ring out.
Lossi plats 10. Tel: (372) 644 3484. Open: daily 8am–7pm (Sat 8pm). Free admission.

Kiek in de Kök

Built in the late 15th century, this tower is 38m (125ft) high and has walls 4m (13ft) thick, and was then the most formidable cannon-tower in northern Europe. The curious name means 'peek in the kitchen', because its height gave the guards a view into kitchens below. It houses an informative exhibition on Tallinn's history, with special emphasis on the fortifications.
Kommandantitee 2. Tel: (372) 644 6686. www.linnamuuseum.ee. Open: Mar–Oct Tue–Sun 10.30am–6pm; Nov–Feb Tue–Sun 10.30am–5pm. Admission charge.

Toomkirik (Cathedral of St Mary the Virgin)

The cathedral dates back to the mid-13th century, with several side chapels and the spire being added later. The airy interior was rebuilt in Baroque style after a fire in 1684. There's a magnificent organ and a large number of heraldic shields. Services are held on Sundays at 10am and organ concerts most Saturdays at noon.
Toom-Kooli 6. Tel: (372) 644 4140. Open: Tue–Sun 9am–3pm. Free admission.

Toompea Loss (Castle)

Toompea Loss presents startlingly different faces from different angles: from Lossi plats it's a pink neoclassical building, but from Toompark (*see pp77, 79*) it's a looming medieval fortress, flaunting the 48m (157ft) tower known as Tall Hermann. Enter the courtyard (only possible on pre-booked group

tours) and you'll see a third aspect, the Riigikogu (Parliament), in National Romantic style, opened in 1922.
Lossi plats 1. Tel: (372) 631 6537. www.riigikogu.ee. Tours: Mon–Fri 10am–4pm. Admission charge. Photo ID required.

Kadriorg

After Vanalinn, Kadriorg is the main draw for visitors to Tallinn. Kadrioru Park is very pleasant, but nothing special in itself; however, it is home to several important attractions, and it's easily reached: tram 1 or 3 from Narva maantee (leave Vanalinn by the Viru gate and go as near as possible straight ahead into Narva maantee: the stop's called Hobujaama) will drop you at the western end of the park. Or just walk; it's about 1.5km (under a mile) from the Viru gate. Narva maantee is uninspiring

but then you bear right onto Weizenbergi street and things improve, with some fine wooden houses and a lot less traffic.

Kadrioru Loss (Kadriorg Palace)

Colourful Kadriorg Palace dates from the time of Peter the Great. It's surrounded by fine formal gardens, and also houses major parts of the national art collection, notably Dutch, German, Italian and Russian paintings from the 16th to the 18th centuries.
Weizenbergi 37. Tel: (372) 606 6400. www.ekm.ee. Open: May–Sept Tue–Sun 10am–5pm; Oct–Apr Wed–Sun 10am–5pm. Admission charge.

KUMU

The Eesti kunstimuuseum (Estonian Art Museum), to give it its full name, was opened in 2006. Half-sunk into the

KUMU is a recent construction, built in 2006

limestone escarpment of Lasnamägi, overlooking Kadrioru Park, it's a startling modern building, designed by Finnish architect Pekka Vapavuori. Its beautifully displayed collections focus on homegrown art.

Weizenbergi 34. Tel: (372) 602 6000. www.ekm.ee. Open: May–Sept Tue–Sun 11am–6pm; Oct–Apr Wed–Sun 11am–6pm. Admission charge.

Lauluväljak (The Song Festival Grounds) Song became a vital expression of nationalism for many people during years of suppression (*see pp84–5*). Tallinn's Song Festival Grounds, with their impressive arch protecting the stage, are a few minutes' walk from Kadrioru Park or KUMU. Apart from the five-yearly song festival, the arena hosts the annual Õllesummer (BeerSummer) rock event. It may be worth noting that if you drop down to the bottom end of the park, below the main arena, you emerge onto the Pirita road, where frequent buses can take you on to Pirita (*see opposite*) or back to the city centre.

Narva mnt 95. Tel: (372) 611 2102. www.lauluvaljak.ee. Open except during special events.

Peeter I majamuseum (Peter the Great's cottage) Sceptics may scoff at the word 'cottage', but this house is remarkably modest, even plain on the outside. Southwest of the Song Festival Grounds, at the southern tip of Kadrioru Park, this was where Peter the Great resided when visiting Tallinn, before the completion of the grander Kadriorg. The preserved interior includes some of his personal belongings.

St Bridget's Convent in Pirita was sacked in 1577

Mäekalda 2. Tel: (372) 601 3136. www.linnamuuseum.ee. Open: May–Aug Tue–Sun 11am–7pm; Sept–Apr Wed–Sun 11am–4pm. Admission charge.

Further afield

Eesti Vabaõhumuuseum (Estonian Open-air Museum)

Attractively set amid forest above the cliffs of Rocca al Mare, this museum displays 72 structures brought and reconstructed from all over Estonia, including farms, houses, a school, wind- and water-mills. You can also take refreshment in an old village inn. To get there, take bus 21 from Balti jaam. (Leave Vanalinn by Nunne street, cross a main road using a subway and then go left to the bus stops.)
Vabaõhumuusemi tee 12. Tel: (372) 654 9100. www.evm.ee. Open: late Apr–Sept daily 10am–8pm (houses 10am–6pm); Oct–mid-Apr daily 10am–5pm. Admission charge.

ARTHUR RANSOME AND THE BALTIC

Arthur Ransome, author of *Swallows and Amazons*, had strong Baltic connections. In 1913 he went to St Petersburg, partly to study Russian folk-tales, partly to escape from a disastrous marriage. Having mastered the language, he became a correspondent for British newspapers and was one of the closest observers of the 1917 Revolutions. He fell in love with Trotsky's secretary, Evgenia Shelepina, and they lived for several years in Tallinn (then called Reval) and Rīga, awaiting Ransome's divorce. A cruise around the Gulf of Finland was immortalised in *Racundra's First Cruise*, which became a yachting classic.

Part of the Estonian Open-air Museum

Pirita

Sandy Pirita is the closest beach to the city, and a centre for various sports; it was the venue for yachting events during the controversial Olympics of 1984. A footpath/cycle track alongside the Pirita road makes it a most attractive destination for cycling, with the classic view of Tallinn's skyline to enjoy on the return leg.

The ruins of **St Bridget's Convent** are well worth a visit. Skeletal against the sky, the walls of the great church are evocative and impressive. The convent was founded in 1407 and sacked under Ivan the Terrible in 1577.
Kloostri tee 9. Tel: (372) 605 5044. www.piritaklooster.ee. Open: Jun–Aug daily 9am–7pm; Apr & May, Sept & Oct daily 10am–6pm; Nov–Mar daily noon–4pm. Admission charge.

The Singing Revolutions

After centuries of foreign rule, the three Baltic republics enjoyed nearly two decades of independence after World War I. However, this was snatched away in the turmoil of 1940 when all three were annexed by the Soviet Union. There followed half a century of Soviet rule, interrupted only by a few years of Nazi occupation from 1941–4.

Soviet rule was at times brutal. Incredibly, Estonia and Latvia are the only European nations whose populations were smaller at the dawn of the 21st century than 100 years previously. This chilling fact testifies to the ravages of war, but even more to mass deportations and the outflow of refugees.

Throughout this time, Estonians, Latvians and Lithuanians clung as best they could to their sense of national identity, and one form in which it could, within limits, be expressed was in song. The Baltics have deep-rooted traditions of song and especially of choral singing, which perhaps fitted in with Soviet notions of collectivity. Festivals of song, though tolerated, were a focus of nationalist emotion. It's

The old KGB headquarters in Vanalinn, Tallinn

The Song Festival Grounds in Tallinn

believed that the five-yearly National Song Festivals have seen the largest choirs ever assembled anywhere.

As the Soviet grip began to weaken, overt protests began around 1987. Mass rallies were resolutely peaceful and usually involved singing. In the following year Estonia's legislative assembly asserted sovereignty, and then declared full independence, though in 1991 a new Soviet crackdown began. But later that year, when hardliners in the Kremlin attempted a coup and were faced down (with Boris Yeltsin at the fore), Soviet control swiftly crumbled, and in the end the transition to independence was almost bloodless.

Estonia's first National Song Festival after independence took place in 1994. Some estimates put the number of people present as around 130,000, which would be almost 10 per cent of the entire population. To put that into perspective, it's like six million people attending Glastonbury or the Last Night of the Proms.

For anyone wishing to learn more about the years of occupation and the transition to independence, both Tallinn and Rīga (see p89) have museums devoted to this subject. *Okupatsioonide Muuseum (Museum of Occupation), Tallinn, Toompea 8. Tel: (372) 668 0250. www.okupatsioon.ee. Open: Tue–Sun 11am–6pm. Admission charge. Lauluväljak (The Song Festival Grounds), Tallinn. Narva mnt 95. Tel: (372) 611 2102. www.lauluvaljak.ee. Open except during special events.*

Saaremaa

Estonia's largest island, Saaremaa, is not yet on the majority of cruise routes, and therein lies much of its appeal. Those who are lucky enough to find a cruise that calls here, or make their own arrangements, find it a perfect antidote to the big-city feel of the regular cruise ports, with a rare combination of unspoiled nature and rich history. Saaremaa's dolomitic limestone supports fertile soils, and in places has been extensively quarried; some notable buildings in St Petersburg, for instance, are faced with Saaremaa stone.

Getting there independently isn't easy, with no scheduled ferries from other countries. There are flights from Tallinn and a few each week from Stockholm. Otherwise it's an overland journey of at least four hours from Tallinn (several buses daily), including a 30-minute ferry crossing to the island of Muhu, linked by bridge to Saaremaa.

FINNISH AND ESTONIAN – THE MYSTERY LANGUAGES

Linguists class almost all Europe's languages, as well as many of south, southwest and central Asia, within the Indo-European family. A conspicuous, and puzzling, exception is the group of languages usually called Finno-Ugric (even the name is controversial). Excepting the isolated example of Hungarian, they are found around the eastern Baltic and in northern regions of Russia. Apart from Finnish and Estonian, they include Sami (Lapp), spoken in the north of Scandinavia and Finland, and Karelian, spoken in Finland and adjoining areas in Russia.

The Bishop's Palace in Kuressaare

Kuressaare

Kuressaare, on the south coast, is Saaremaa's only town, with a well-preserved old quarter. Popular with artists, it has several interesting galleries.

Kuressaare Piiskopilinnus (The Bishop's Castle) There are many medieval castles around the Baltic, but Piiskopilinnus is unique in having no later additions or alterations; essentially, it looks as it did when new, in the late 14th century. It's built to a square plan, with two towers on the north side, flanking the entrance. The courtyard is surrounded by vaulted galleries. The castle now houses the island's museum, which explores both historical and natural sides of Saaremaa.

Lossihoov tn 1. Tel: (045) 54463.
www.saaremaamuuseum.ee.
Open: May–Aug daily 10am–6pm;
Sept–Apr daily 11am–6pm.
Admission charge.

Beyond Kuressaare

Kaali Meteorite Crater About 18km
(11 miles) east of Kuressaare, this
meteorite crater is around 110m
(360ft) in overall diameter, with a
central, almost perfectly circular, lake
about 50m (165ft) across. Geologists
have concluded that it was formed
around 700 BC.

Panga Island tradition names Panga
Cliff, on the north coast, a place of
power, with tales of ritual and sacrifice.
Even in the 1930s it's said that
fishermen would pour offerings of beer
into the waves to ensure a calm sea and
a good catch.

Sõrve Peninsula The peninsula extends
around 32km (20 miles); its tip is less
than 30km (19 miles) from the Latvian
coast. It saw fierce fighting in World
War II, and there are extensive remains
of massive Soviet defences known as
Stebel's Battery. The sandy point at the
extreme end of the peninsula is a wild,
often windswept, spot with a tall,
slender lighthouse.

Muhu

Koguva Koguva is considered Estonia's
best-preserved village. Most of its
buildings date from the 19th century,
with some earlier ones in the village
centre. The massive drystone walls are
over 200 years old.

The circular lake at the centre of Kaali Meteorite Crater

LATVIA

The central and largest of the Baltic republics, Latvia shares with its neighbours a long and often troubled history, for most of which it has been dominated by external powers. Its interwar independence lasted little more than 20 years; it's strange to reflect that it will beat that record as soon as 2012.

Rīga

Rīga, 800 years old in 2001, is immensely proud of its history but certainly not backward looking. Here, more than most, you get a sense of a city that's been busy rediscovering itself. Rīga currently claims to be Europe's 'party capital', but such ephemeral 'honours' pale beside its enduring qualities, especially its rich and diverse architectural heritage, symbolised by the beguiling skyline that greets incoming vessels.

Approaches

Ships from Helsinki or St Petersburg round the Estonian island of Saaremaa, while those from the west will skirt the peninsula of Latvia's western province before entering a huge sheltered bay. These low coasts vanish from sight before sandy beaches backed with pine forests appear ahead. Rīga lies 10km (6 miles) inland, along the broad Daugava River.

Cruise ships berth just below the first bridge, Vanšu tilts. The spires of Vecrīga (Old Rīga) are easily visible and its labyrinth of narrow streets starts within five minutes' walk. Some key Art Nouveau streets lie equally close, albeit in a different direction. To link into public transport, walk a couple of

The approach to Latvia's capital, Rīga

The Baltic republics

Rīgas Dome has been greatly extended over the years

unmissable museum, bearing witness to the half-century of Soviet occupation (and a few years under German control). Historical records, personal stories and photographs are supplemented by artefacts from weapons to propaganda posters. *Strēlnieku laukums 1. Tel: (067) 212 715. www.occupationmuseum.lv. Open: May–Sept daily 11am–6pm (Wed 7pm); Oct–Apr Tue–Sun 11am–5pm. Donations requested.*

blocks to Kronvalda bulvaris to find tram No 7.

Vecrīga (Old Rīga)

There's a lot packed into Rīga's compact Old Town. Its seemingly random layout means that first-timers are almost guaranteed to get pleasurably lost, but that only encourages discovery. Architecturally it's a joyous medley, with outstanding medieval buildings rubbing shoulders with neoclassical, Art Nouveau and unashamed modern and, generally, getting along just fine.

Vehicular access to Vecrīga is limited, but it's not just a museum piece; the Parliament and several government departments are here. Numerous cafés, bars and restaurants are busy with locals as well as tourists.

Latvijas Okupācijas muzejs (Museum of the Occupation of Latvia)

A stark slab of a building, plonked incongruously next to the House of Blackheads, houses a sombre but

Melngalvju nams (House of Blackheads)

This is in fact a replica – the original was flattened by bombing in 1941 – but it's a very convincing one, and symbolises the city's renewal. Its crow-stepped, colourful façades are among Rīga's most photographed sites (the light's better in the afternoon). The original building existed before 1334, and the curious name refers to a merchants' guild that had similar establishments in several Hanseatic cities. Today, it houses a restaurant, tourist information centre and museum. *Rātsaukums 6. Tel: (067) 044 300. Open: May–Sept daily 10am–5pm; Oct–Apr daily 11am–5pm. Admission charge.*

Rīgas Dome (Cathedral)

Established in 1211, much extended in the 14th and 15th centuries, the present cathedral is largely a brick structure in Gothic style. When it was completed in 1884, the organ was the world's largest, boasting 6,718 pipes from 8mm (⅓ inch) to a

(Cont. on p92)

Walk: Art Nouveau ramblings

Rīga is reckoned to have over 800 Art Nouveau buildings; to visit them all in a single walk would be a tall order indeed. This itinerary takes in a fair sample of the finest, but real buffs should consult one of the specialist guidebooks that are readily obtainable in Rīga.

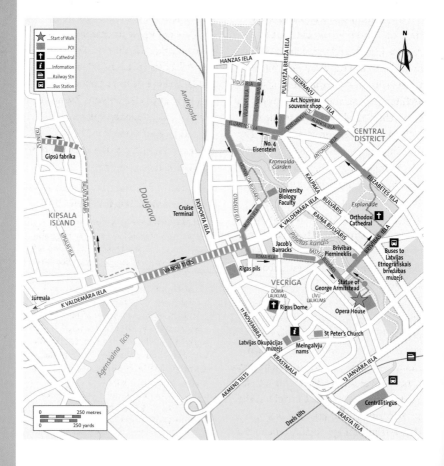

Start in front of the Opera House. Bear right towards a canal then walk alongside it, passing the statue of George Armitstead, Mayor of Rīga between 1901 and 1912. Cross the next bridge and walk past **Brīvības Piemineklis** (Freedom Monument; see p92).

Follow Brīvības iela to the Orthodox Cathedral, and perhaps have a look inside; otherwise turn left to the centre of the park (Esplanāde) then go right to meet Elizabetes iela. Go left and cross busy K Valdemāra iela.

Where Elizabetes iela bends left, go right on Antonijas iela then left on Alberta iela, its right side lined with flamboyant buildings by Mikhail Eisenstein, Rīga's leading Jugendstil architect. At the end, the walk turns left on Strēlnieku iela, but just to the right is the Art Nouveau souvenir shop. The blue building at No 4, another Eisenstein, was originally a school.

Back at Elizabetes iela, turn right and right again into Pulkveža Brieža iela; go about 100m (110yds) up here, taking in its impressive Nouveau Gothic buildings, then return to Elizabetes iela. Take the next right on Rūpniecības iela, left on Vidus iela and left again on Vīlandes iela: walk on the right side to appreciate the façades on the left, especially No 10. No 4 is lovely but faded. Rejoin Elizabetes iela and turn right, then go left on Kronvalda bulvāris.

Cross over a canal then bear left into the Kronvalda Garden. Go right at the second fork. Pass a yellow building (University Biology Faculty) then turn immediately right. Cross Kronvalda bulvāris, follow Muitas iela opposite, then go second left on Citadeles iela.

Cross K Valdemāra iela and you're back in the Old Town. The quickest way back to the start is to bear left on Toma iela then right on Basteja bulvāris.

An interesting extension to the walk, giving different perspectives on Rīga, would be to turn right instead of crossing K Valdemāra iela. Cross Vanšu tilts (Vanšu Bridge) to Kipsala Island and then go right, following the shoreline opposite the cruise quay.

There are many interesting wooden houses here, old and new. Turn left at Gipsū fabrika (plasterworks), now in residential use. It has a pleasant café. A couple of blocks down is Zvenieku iela: No 5 is a Jugendstil gem.

Retrace your steps from here, enjoying the views of the spires of the Old Town as you return.

ART NOUVEAU

Art nouveau is French for 'new art'; the German term *Jugendstil* ('youth style') is also used. The movement blossomed between 1890 and World War I. Characterised by flowing, organic forms, often directly imitating plants, and hugely important in the applied and decorative arts, its grandest and most permanent expressions are in architecture.

Rīga has the greatest collection of Jugendstil buildings in Europe; Helsinki also has a marvellous assemblage. Perhaps the most complete Art Nouveau city is Ålesund in Norway, rebuilt after a fire in 1904. The UK's finest examples are in Glasgow, where Charles Rennie Mackintosh was the chief protagonist of the style.

mighty 10m (33ft) long. Alongside there's a pleasant cloister whose central garden has been restored in monastic style. Artefacts displayed here include an enigmatic stone head and a wonderful cockerel weathervane.
1 Doma laukums. Tel: (067) 356 699. http://doms.lv. Open: May–Sept daily 10am–6pm (Wed & Fri 5pm); Oct–Apr daily 10am–5pm. Admission charge.

Rīgas pils (Castle) The nearest bit of Vecrīga to the cruise quay, the castle is unlikely to be missed. It's well worth a glance, but is not open to the public – it's the president's official residence. Wander up onto the Vanšu bridge and peek into the Presidential Garden.

An Art Nouveau motif in the Central District

St Peter's Church Tallest of Rīga's spires, St Peter's has an observation platform at 70m (230ft) offering a fabulous view over Vecrīga and beyond. There's a lift to ease the climb. Don't miss the interior, though, which is tall, spare and simple.
19 Skārņu iela. Tel: (067) 229 426. Open: daily 10am–6pm. Admission charge.

Central District
The modern city is centred north and east of Vecrīga, the demarcation being emphasised by some pleasant parks and the Pilsētas Canal. Where Brīvības iela crosses this you'll find **Brīvības Piemineklis** (Freedom Monument), 42m (138ft) tall and a key symbol of Latvia's struggles for independence.

The Central District has interesting museums and galleries, but its biggest attraction for most visitors is the profusion of Art Nouveau buildings; for more on these *see pp90–91*.

Shops and markets
'Old and new' Rīga are embodied just southeast of Vecrīga; cross a busy intersection by a subway. To the left is the spanking new **Stockmann** department store. Beyond the railway tracks are the vast hangars of **Centrālitirgus (Central Market)**, one of Europe's largest. The left-hand building is devoted to meat, and in between there's an open-air market for flowers, fruit and vegetables. In the larger building are all manner of specialities,

Summer flowers at the Latvian Ethnographic Open-air Museum

from cheap clothes to fabulous local honey and beeswax products.
Tel: (067) 229 985. Open: hours vary for different areas: see www.rct.lv

Latvijas etnogrāfiskais brīvdabas muzejs (Latvian Ethnographic Open-air Museum)

There are open-air museums all round the Baltic, but this is one of the very best. The recreated villages and homesteads are dispersed though 80ha (200 acres) of lovely forest, full of birdsong in spring and summer. On the smaller paths you can forget you're in a museum at all. The museum has 118 buildings; at weekends and in high summer most of them are open and there are live craft demonstrations as

well, but at any time it's a pleasure to wander around, and there will always be some interiors open to explore. Bus No 1 from Brīvības iela takes about 25 minutes.
440 Brīvības gatve. Tel: (067) 799 4106. www.ltg.lv. Open: daily 10am–5pm. Admission charge.

Jūrmala

If you need a beach fix, head for Jūrmala, about 25km (16 miles) away; get there absurdly cheaply by train or minibus. Its 32km (20 miles) of white-sand beaches have areas to suit most tastes. Majori and Bulduri have Blue Flag status, making them a good choice for bathing, while Pumpuri is the place for kite- and wind-surfing.

Klaipėda's Old Town is a collection of narrow streets and squares

LITHUANIA

As a cruise destination, Lithuania currently ranks last among the Baltic nations, suffering somewhat from a relatively short coastline, while its handsome and lively capital, Vilnius, stands around 300km (185 miles) inland. The small modern nation is but a remnant of what was, in medieval times, the largest state in Europe. It later formed a commonwealth with Poland but, as this declined, surrounding countries claimed its territory. Lithuania regained independence in 1919 but was annexed by Stalin in 1940. Renewed independence in 1991 led rapidly to membership of the EU and NATO.

Klaipėda

Lithuania's main port, Klaipėda is the country's oldest city, founded in the 13th century. For much of its history it was a German possession, known as Memelburg, but was seized by Lithuania in 1923. These mixed influences make it a fascinating place. The lengthy waterfront has a largely industrial character but there are plans to transform much of it. The adjacent resorts of Nida and Palanga, with their sandy beaches and forested surroundings, along with Kuršių Nerija (Curonian Spit), are developing rapidly as a kind of Baltic Riviera.

Approaches

From any approach, Lithuania presents a straight, sandy coastline, apparently unbroken until the ship enters the narrow channel separating the mainland from Kuršių Nerija. The cruise terminal is within a 500m (550yd) walk of the centre, which is split by the Dangė River; the Old Town is on the south bank.

Klaipėda New Town

North of the river, the 'New' Town is by no means all modern, with many examples of neo-Gothic architecture, most notably the red-brick **Central Post Office** on Liepu gatvė. Alongside is the 44m (144ft) **Carillon**, whose 48 bells are rung at noon on Saturday and Sunday.

Klaipėda Old Town

Little remains of the great **Memelburg Fortress**, but an isolated, moated bastion can be found east of the Old Town. The Old Town itself is an attractive place of narrow streets; German influence is evident in many of its buildings. Its focal point is **Teatro aikštė** (Theatre Square), dominated by the 19th-century **Drama Theatre**.

Nearby, **Kalvystės Muziejus** (Blacksmith Museum) includes a working forge as well as many fine examples of metalcraft.
Šaltkalvių 2. Tel: (046) 410 526.
Open: Tue–Sat 10am–5.30pm.
Admission charge.

Mažosios Lietuvos istorijos muziejus (Historical Museum of Lithuania Minor)

This is of great cultural interest: Lithuania Minor is the region south of Klaipėda, most of which is now incorporated in the Kaliningrad Oblast of Russia. The wooden building is fascinating in itself.
Didžioji Vandens 6. Tel: (046) 410 524.
www.mlimuziejus.lt. Open: Tue–Sat 10am–5.30pm. Admission charge.

Kuršių Nerija (Curonian Spit)

An extraordinary natural phenomenon and a World Heritage Site, the Spit is a sliver of sand dunes 98km (61 miles) long and never more than 4km (2½ miles) wide – in places barely 400m (440yds) – which shelters a huge lagoon. Half its length is in Lithuania, its landward end belonging to Russia (Kaliningrad). Frequent ferries make the short crossing from Klaipėda and, while you can easily walk to the shore, the best beaches and amenities are further south, best accessed by bicycle or hail-and-ride minibuses. You should note that permits (easily available) are needed if you intend to travel as far as Neringa.

Poland

Baltic history is turbulent, and Poland's more turbulent than most. From the 14th to the 16th centuries it was a great power, both in its own right and in alliance with Lithuania, but vanished from the map in 1795, dissected by Austria, Prussia and Russia. Brief independence from 1918 ended with the Nazi invasion, which precipitated World War II. Poland then became a Soviet satellite, before the collapse of Communism in 1989. It became an EU member in 2004.

GDYNIA AND GDAŃSK

Gdynia and Gdańsk, along with Sopot, which lies in between, are known as Trójmiasto (TriCity). Gdynia was created from almost nothing between the wars to become a major port, and is the main cruise port. Sopot is a pleasant resort, with a fine beach. Gdańsk, where some cruise ships berth, is the real draw, from its splendid Old Town to its great shipyards, the cradle of Solidarity, the trade union

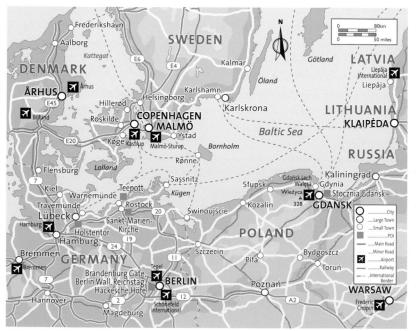

Dar Pomorza is moored at the waterfront in the centre of Gdynia

organisation that became a movement for social change (*see p98*).

Gdynia

Its creation in the 1920s and 1930s makes Gdynia fascinating for architecture buffs. For everyone else, interest is heavily concentrated along the waterfront. Many cruise ships berth at Nabrzeże Pomorskie, right in the heart of things.

Akwarium Gdyńskie

At the seaward end of Nabrzeże Pomorskie, this is a combined aquarium, with both exotic and native species, and an oceanographic museum. The Baltic Room features a giant relief map of the Baltic seabed.
Al Jana Pawła II 1. Tel: (058) 732 66 01. www.aquarium.gdynia.pl.

Open: Jun–Aug daily 9am–8pm; Apr, May & Sept daily 9am–7pm; Oct–Mar daily 10am–6pm.

Dar Pomorza

This white frigate is the grandest of several ships moored at Nabrzeże Pomorskie. Built in 1909, she served as a training ship for over 50 years.
Nabrzeże Pomorskie. Tel: (058) 620 23 71. www.cmm.pl. Open: Jun–Aug daily 9am–6pm; Sept–Nov & Feb–May Tue–Sun 10am–4pm.

Gdańsk

A leading Hanseatic city, Gdańsk has remained a major port ever since. For long periods it was a free city, including from 1918 to 1939, when it was known by its German name, Danzig. Frequent trains link Gdynia and Gdańsk. The port is about 4km (2½ miles) north of the city centre.

Centralne Muzeum Morskie (Central Maritime Museum)

A little shuttle ferry crosses the river to the main site of the Maritime Museum, which occupies three historic granaries. Varied exhibitions depict Poland's long, proud seafaring traditions.
Ołowianka 9–13. Tel: (058) 301 86 11. www.cmm.pl. Open: Jul & Aug daily 10am–6pm; Sept–Nov & Feb–Jun Tue–Sun 10am–4pm; Dec & Jan Tue–Sun 10am–3pm. Admission charge. Combined tickets cover the museum, Żuraw and the ship Sołdek.

Historic Gdańsk

Gdańsk has three separate historic quarters, the largest being **Główne Miasto** (Main Town). Painstakingly restored after the ravages of war, it again looks much as it did three or four hundred years ago. Streets are lined by tall houses with ornate gables and colourful façades, nowhere finer than along **ul Długa** (Long Street). At its east end is the **Town Hall**, with its 80m (265ft) tower; inside is the fascinating **Muzeum Historycznego Miasta Gdańska** (Historical Museum).

Beyond the Town Hall are **Fontanna Neptuna** (Neptune's Fountain), a symbol of Gdańsk since 1633, and **Długi Targ** (Long Market), now a focus of street life, lined with bars and restaurants.

A poem by Czesław Miłosz on the monument to the fallen workers

SOLIDARITY AND LECH WAŁĘSA

Lech Wałęsa (b. 1943) was an electrician at Gdańsk's Lenin Shipyard. He became a member of a strike committee there in 1970, which was illegal under Communist rule. After ten more years of activism, in 1980 Wałęsa became a founder, and de facto leader, of Solidarność (Solidarity), a 'free trade union' that campaigned for political and economic change. This became a broader political movement, which eventually – after having been suppressed under martial law – triumphed in semi-free elections in 1989, entering a coalition that formed the Soviet bloc's first non-Communist government. Elected president in 1990, Wałęsa attracted criticism for his political style, and narrowly missed re-election in 1995, though his popularity waned rapidly after this. In 1983 Wałęsa was awarded the Nobel Peace Prize.

Długi Targ leads to an attractive waterfront; follow this north to **Żuraw** (Crane), two brick towers supporting a huge wooden hoist, once driven by treadmill, which doubled as a city gate. It dates back to 1444.

Town Hall, ul Długa 46/47. Tel: (058) 310 12 014. Open: Jun–Aug daily 10am–5pm; Sept–May Tue–Sun 10am–4pm.
Żuraw, ul Szeroka 67/68.
Tel: (058) 301 69 38. www.cmm.pl.
Open: Jul & Aug daily 10.30am–6.30pm; Sept–Nov & Feb–Apr Tue–Fri 10am–4pm, Sat & Sun 10.30am–4.30pm; Dec & Jan Tue–Fri 10am–3pm, Sat & Sun 10am–3.30pm. Admission charge.

Stocznia Gdańsk (Gdańsk Shipyard)

As the birthplace of Solidarity, the shipyard is a pivotal historic site.

Run-down and rather ghostly now, it's been partly colonised by artists. In front of the main gate is Solidarity Square, and a monument to the fallen workers of the 1970 strikes in the form of three 42m (138ft) high crosses, built by yard workers. Inside the gate is the fascinating **Solidarity Museum**. *Ul Doki 1. Tel: (058) 769 292. Open: Tue–Sun 10am–6pm. Free admission.*

View across the historic Główne Miasto of Gdańsk

Germany

It's easy to imagine that Germany has always been there, but it's only existed as a nation-state since 1871. It was occupied by the victorious Allies between 1945 and 1949 and was then divided until reunification in 1990. Having dominated European history for all the wrong reasons in the first half of the 20th century, Germany has since striven to redeem itself, its commitment to European cooperation being the most obvious sign of this.

Rostock and Warnemünde are 12km (7½ miles) apart (*see map on p96*), with frequent train and bus connections. Warnemünde is the cruise port, but the 800-year-old Hanseatic town of Rostock is the main attraction.

Warnemünde's new cruise centre is handily located next to the railway station and a few minutes from the town centre and seafront.

Rostock

Rostock's extensive Old Town lends itself to exploratory wanderings: several specific sights really shouldn't be missed.

One of these is the massive **Sankt-Marien-Kirche** (St Mary's Church), which dates to the 14th century. Its great wonder is its **Astronomische Uhr**, an astronomical clock from 1472, which has worked non-stop since 1643; the Apostles emerge daily at noon.

Sankt-Petri-Kirche (St Peter's Church) has a 117m (384ft) tower. Rebuilt after World War II, it has a grand view of the city.

Seat of the town council for almost 800 years, the medieval **Rathaus** (Town Hall) has a seven-towered Gothic façade with an 18th-century Baroque extension oddly grafted on its front.

The beautiful **Kloster zum Heiligen Kreuz** (Holy Cross Convent), with its lovingly restored decorated vaulting, houses the **Kulturhistorisches Museum** (Cultural History Museum).

Sankt-Marien-Kirche, Am Ziegenmarkt 4. Tel: (0381) 492 33 96. Open: May–Sept Mon–Sat 10am–6pm, Sun 11.15am–5pm; Oct–Apr Mon–Sat 10am–12.15pm & 2–4pm, Sun 11am–12.15pm.

Sankt-Petri-Kirche (tower), Alter Markt. Tel: (0381) 492 33 96.

www.petrikirche-rostock.de.

Open: Jun–Aug Mon–Fri 10am–7pm, Sat & Sun 10am–5pm; Sept & Oct, Apr & May daily 10am–5pm; Nov–Mar Mon–Fri 10am–4pm, Sat & Sun 10am–5pm. Admission charge.

Kloster zum Heiligen Kreuz, Klosterhof. Tel: (0381) 20 35 90. Open: Tue–Sun 10am–6pm. Free admission.

Excursion to Berlin

When Rostock itself is so intriguing, travelling two to three hours each way to Berlin may seem like trying to cram too much in, yet this is a standard cruise excursion. And Berlin is a great city, busy celebrating its post-reunification renaissance: highlights include the symbolic Brandenburg Gate, the remains of the Berlin Wall, the stunning new glass dome of the Reichstag and the restored courtyards of Hackesche Höfe, not to mention some of Europe's best shopping – and around 7,000 bars and restaurants! But still, it's like 'doing' London as a day-trip from Cardiff.

Warnemünde

Warnemünde has a large marina, sandy beaches, an enticing Old Town and plentiful cafés and restaurants. The skyline is dominated by the 31m (102ft) high **Leuchtturm** (Lighthouse), built in 1897. Its galleries offer great panoramic views.

Alongside is the Modernist pavilion known as the **Teepott** (Teapot), which now houses a popular restaurant and a museum devoted to explorer Reinhold Kasten.

Leuchtturm. Tel: (0381) 519 26 26.
Open: daily 10am–7pm.
Admission charge.
Teepott. www.gna-net.de.
Open: daily 10am–6pm.
Admission charge for museum.

Travemünde

The modern, deep-water port of Travemünde handles the main cruise and ferry traffic. A pleasant seaside town with a busy ferry trade, Travemünde's great landmark is the

Kröpeliner Strasse in Rostock's Old Town

Germany

four-masted barque *Passat*, which was built in 1911 and is said to have rounded Cape Horn no fewer than 39 times; her masts reach 56m (184ft) above the water.
Tel: (0451) 122 52 02. Open: mid-May–mid-Sept daily 10am–5pm; Easter–mid-May & mid-Sept–Oct Sat & Sun 11am–4.30pm. Closed: Nov–Easter. Admission charge.

Lübeck

Hanseatic cities are plentiful around the Baltic, but Lübeck is *the* Hanseatic city, and the **Innenstadt**, the Old Town, is a medieval marvel (recognised in its entirety as a World Heritage Site). Numerous churches, warehouses and merchants' residences line the streets. Along its western waterfront are moored a dozen historic ships, representing most stages of Lübeck's maritime history.

Buddenbrookhaus

Commemorates the brothers Heinrich and Thomas Mann, both noted novelists: Thomas won the Nobel Prize for the Lübeck-inspired *Buddenbrooks*. *Mengstrasse. Tel: (0451) 122 41 90. www.buddenbrookhaus.de. Open: Apr–Dec daily 10am–6pm; Jan–Mar daily 10am–5pm. Admission charge.*

Dom zu Lübeck (Cathedral)

This is the oldest church in Lübeck, much of it 12th-century; its slender twin spires are almost as emblematic as the Holstentor (*see opposite*). *Mühlendamm. Tel: (0451) 747 04. www.domzuluebeck.de. Open: Apr–Oct daily 10am–6pm; Nov–Mar daily 10am–4pm. Free admission.*

Drägerhaus und Behnhaus

Adjoining merchant mansions feature magnificent interiors from *c.* 1800, and

The Dom zu Lübeck and rooftops

display paintings from Caspar David Friedrich and Edvard Munch.

Königstrasse. Tel: (0451) 122 41 48. Open: Apr–Dec daily 10am–5pm; Jan–Mar Tue–Sun 11am–5pm. Admission charge.

Heiligen-Geist-Hospital (Hospital of the Holy Spirit)

A grand medieval building and almshouse with a magnificent vaulted hall that can be visited. It also hosts special events.

Am Koberg. Tel: (0451) 122 20 40. Open: Apr–Dec daily 10am–5pm; Jan–Mar Tue–Sun 11am–5pm. Free admission.

Holstentor

The symbol of Lübeck is the Holstein Gate, a twin-towered 15th-century fortification. It houses an interesting museum dedicated to merchant life.

Tel: (0451) 122 41 29. Open: Apr–Dec daily 10am–6pm; Jan–Mar daily 11am–5pm. Admission charge.

Rathaus (Town Hall)

Developed in the 13th century from three majestic houses, whose gables still form part of the façade, Lübeck's Town Hall is one of the oldest and finest in Germany.

Tel: (0451) 122 10 05. Tours: Mon–Fri 11am, noon, 3pm. Free admission.

Sankt-Marien-Kirche (St Mary's Church)

The prime church of the Hanseatic League is the third largest in Germany, an exemplar of Gothic brick

The Holstentor in Lübeck

construction. Composer Dietrich Buxtehude was organist and choirmaster here for 40 years from 1667.

Schüsselbuden. Tel: (0451) 773 91. Open: Apr–Sept daily 10am–6pm; Oct daily 10am–5pm; Nov–Mar daily 10am–4pm. Free admission.

Sankt-Petri-Kirche (St Peter's Church)

Another magnificent church, Romanesque with Gothic additions, but perhaps its prime attraction is the view from the tower over the wonderful roofscape of the Innenstadt.

Schmiedestrasse. Tel: (0451) 397 73 20. Open (tower): Apr–Sept daily 9am–9pm; Oct–Mar 10am–7pm (extended during Christmas market). Admission charge.

Excursion to Hamburg

Lübeck to Hamburg is only 45 minutes by train, a more sensible proposition than Rostock to Berlin. A cosmopolitan port and economic powerhouse, yet laced with green spaces, it's certainly impressive, while the Reeperbahn has the allure of notoriety. But if you only have one day, why not spend it in Lübeck?

The Hanseatic League

Even the most casual traveller around the Baltic is bound to come across mention of the Hanseatic League (or Hansa). The Hansa has been described as the world's first multinational corporation, but this is potentially misleading. Multinational it certainly was, but it was not a corporation, certainly not in any modern sense. Rather, it was an association or confederation of merchants or guilds of merchants.

Although they might be competitors in business, merchants recognised common interest in the general furtherance of trade, and in the need for protection against bandits and pirates, travelled in large parties by land and combined to use large ships or convoys by sea. The Hanseatic League originated in the 12th century with an agreement between merchants in Hamburg and Lübeck, which soon proved beneficial to both.

Seeing this, merchants in other cities sought to join the alliance: Cologne, for instance, joined in 1201. As the League grew, it came to monopolise trade in the Baltic and to take large shares elsewhere, for instance in the North Sea and on the Rhine. It employed its own fighting ships and soldiers (often mercenaries), not just for protection against pirates but to enforce its own monopoly on power; in the 14th century the League entered into a war against the Danish King Waldemar IV and ultimately emerged victorious. The ensuing Treaty of Stralsund (1370) enshrined a Hansa monopoly over most Scandinavian trade.

This perhaps marked the zenith of the Hansa, which waged other successful campaigns before a defeat by the Dutch in 1441. Its decline thereafter was protracted but inexorable. National governments were growing in power while the Hansa was plagued by internal dissent. The last meeting of the Hansa's governing body, the Diet, was held in 1669. However, the League has never been formally wound up, and to this day Hamburg, Bremen and Lübeck still lay claim to the title of 'Free and Hanseatic City'.

Lübeck was the centre of the Hansa throughout its history. It capitalised on its favourable geographical position between the Baltic and the great central European trade routes, and also benefited from its status as a free city. This meant that it had no overlord and was answerable only to

A cog ship in the harbour at Malmö; these wooden ships were often used to transport goods in the era of the Hanseatic League

the Holy Roman Emperor. Gdańsk – then known as Danzig – enjoyed similar status.

Over the centuries a fluctuating number of cities were members of the Hansa or had looser association with it; the maximum number of members was somewhere over 150. Most of the major ports around the Baltic were members for at least part of the Hanseatic period. Visby, the leading Baltic port before the rise of the Hansa, enjoyed a somewhat ambivalent relationship with the League and was slow to align itself.

Cities such as Rīga and Tallinn (originally called Reval) were founded or developed by German settlers under the aegis of the Hansa. It's only newer cities like St Petersburg (founded 1703) that have no Hanseatic connections.

The Hansa had outposts – called *kontore* – in cities as far afield as Novgorod in Russia, Bergen in Norway, and London. Many other ports on England's east coast (and also Bristol) had Hanseatic representatives. A Hanseatic warehouse still stands in King's Lynn.

Denmark

Denmark is the smallest of the Baltic nations by area; about a third is made up of islands and nowhere is more than about 50km (30 miles) from the sea. The coastline is long and convoluted, while inland Denmark is low-lying, green and intensively cultivated. In the medieval period it was one of the great powers of the region, dominating the triple kingdom with Sweden and Norway. Modern Denmark is prosperous, peaceful and forward-looking, yet treasures its rich history.

COPENHAGEN (KØBENHAVN)

More than a quarter of Denmark's population live in the Copenhagen area, but its dominance is relatively new; nearby Roskilde and Helsingør both claimed pre-eminence before the Reformation, when Copenhagen became the capital. Today, easy communications across the Øresund bring ever-closer ties with Malmö in Sweden, and the two function almost as one dynamic metropolis. Copenhagen, with its intimate lanes and vast cold palaces, is a city of shifting perspectives. Its public transport system is excellent and it is one of the best cities in the world for cycling, so getting around is never a problem. And it's that rare thing, a great port where the water is clean enough for swimming

Approaches

From Oslo or Göteborg, the approach runs through the Øresund narrows, between Helsingør and Helsingborg, giving excellent views of Kronborg Slot (Elsinore Castle; see p114), and also passing the island of Ven, where the astronomer Tycho Brahe (1546–1601) had his legendary observatory, Uraniborg.

From the south, ships enter the Øresund under the impressive bridge linking Denmark and Sweden. Malmö's Turning Torso (see p41) is another dominant landmark. The northern and southern approaches unite at the mouth of the harbour, almost on the point of docking.

The waterfront

Cruise ships moor at Langeliniekaj, where there's a pleasant parade of shops and cafés, only a few minutes' walk from **Den Lille Havfrue** (the Little Mermaid). For one of Copenhagen's 'must-sees', she's surprisingly small and inconspicuous, but perhaps this adds poignancy. Inspired by a Hans Christian Andersen story, the statue was made by Edvard Eriksen in 1913.

Many water-borne tours of Copenhagen are available, but a quicker and cheaper alternative is to take one of the harbour bus-boats from Nordre Toldbod, a short way south of Den Lille Havfrue. Crossing to the eastern shore, the second stop is **Operaen** (the Opera House), its amazing flying roof making it Copenhagen's most striking modern building. Sample the architecture by visiting the foyer and café. There are tours in English, for pre-booked groups only.

The next stop, back on the west shore, is another iconic new building, **Det Kongelige Teater** (Royal Danish Playhouse). Just round the corner is **Nyhavn** (New Harbour). This narrow channel, dating from the late 17th century, brought ships to the heart of the city. Warehouses and merchants' dwellings sprang up and most of them are still there, the colourful façades on the sunny north side making a particularly attractive scene. Many now house cafés and restaurants and the wharf is lined with outdoor seating.

(*Cont. on p110*)

Tour: Copenhagen by bike

Many experts rate Copenhagen the world's best city for cycling. A culture in which cycling was already popular has been supported by dedicated work by the city authorities to improve the network of bike lanes and traffic signals.

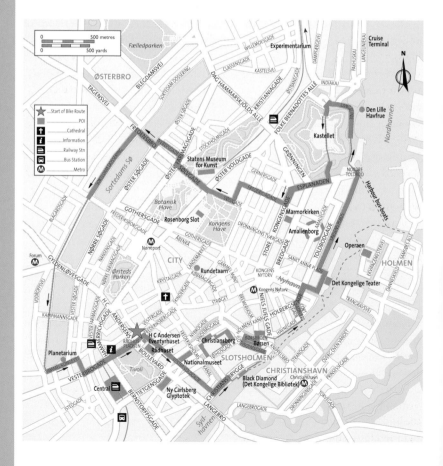

Even if you might hesitate to cycle through city streets at home, Copenhagen feels safe and encouraging. There are bike lanes on virtually every street and you'll soon see that cycling here is not the preserve of a Lycra-clad coterie. All sorts of people ride bikes: stockbrokers in suits, girls in short skirts and high heels, grandparents and youngsters. It almost feels a shame to suggest just one route. However, the following is a simple tour that takes in many of the main sights and links some green spaces.

Observe the designated bike lanes, and always ride on the right, just like other traffic. Traffic signals at intersections always give plenty of time for cyclists. Don't ride on pedestrianised streets or in parks, even if you see other people doing so.

Start from **Rådhuspladsen** (Town Hall Square; *see p111*); follow Vester Voldgade, with the Rådhuset on your right, to reach Christians Brygge, on the **waterfront** (*see p107*). Go left here and soon you can leave the road and follow the water's edge. Continue past the **Black Diamond** (*see p110*) until you have to rejoin the road.

Take the next left into Slothsolmsgade, then first right, at the near end of the remarkable **Børsen** building (*see p110*). Use the crossings to get onto the bridge, Børsbroen, cross it and go along the waterfront again.

Turn third left on Cort Adelers Gade, then right on Holbergsgade and cross the bridge at **Nyhavn** (*see p107*). Turn right and follow the waterfront round to

pass the new **Det Kongelige Teater** (*see p107*). Look across, too, to the amazing **Operaen** (*see p107*).

Continue along the waterfront (Larsens Plads), passing access to **Amalienborg** (*see p112*). At the end of this section you're steered slightly away from the water. Go under a bridge and ride alongside the moat of **Kastellet** (*see p112*). Soon you can rejoin the harbour front again, and crowds tell you you're approaching **Den Lille Havfrue** (*see p107*).

Follow the road round left (you're very close to the cruise terminal at this point). Where it bends right leave it at a crossing. Walk down steps and cross a narrow bridge into Kastellet. Ride through here by the straightest course and emerge into Esplanaden. Turn right, take the second main left on Store Kongensgade, then third right on Fredericiagade. Turn left at the end, then right. The road runs alongside the wall of **Kongens Have** (*see p112*) and you could go in to look at **Rosenborg Slot** (*see p112*).

Follow crowds of other cyclists across a busy junction; **Statens Museum for Kunst** (*see p113*) is on your right. Where the road splits keep right, then bear immediately left again into Webersgade. Cross Fredensbro and the city's ring of lakes. Turn left and follow the shoreline of the string of lakes to its end.

Turn left on Gammel Kongevej. Pass the striking Planetarium and then turn right to Vesterbrogade, which leads back to Rådhuspladsen.

The harbour bus continues to a third waterfront icon, the **Black Diamond**. Everyone calls it this, though officially it's an extension to **Det Kongelige Bibliotek** (The Royal Library).

Slotsholmen and the south of the city

The Black Diamond stands on the shores of Slotsholmen, a small island defined by canals, which is the heart of the original city. It is crammed with museums and other sites of interest, and several more lie just to the west.

Børsen

Arguably Slotsholmen's most beautiful building, the former Stock Exchange was built in the 17th century in Dutch Renaissance style. Observe the spire, formed by the twisted tails of four dragons.
Not open to the public.
Metro: Kongens Nytorv.

The Black Diamond on the waterfront

Christiansborg

This palace, the fifth on the site, was completed in 1928. It's anything but homely, and has never been a royal residence, but does host State receptions. It houses the Folketing (Parliament), government offices and the Supreme Court.
Slotsholmen. Tel: (033) 92 64 92.
www.ses.dk. Tours available May–Sept daily 10am–6pm; Oct–Apr Tue–Sun 10am–6pm. Admission charge.
Metro: Kongens Nytorv.

Nationalmuseet

The National Museum tells the story of Denmark's land and people, from prehistory to the present. Denmark's links with Greenland make the ethnographical section one of the world's premier collections on the peoples of the Arctic.
Ny Vestergade 10. Tel: (033) 13 44 11.
www.natmus.dk. Open: Tue–Sun 10am–5pm. Free admission.
Metro: Kongens Nytorv.

Ny Carlsberg Glyptotek

Founded by Carl Jacobsen of the Carlsberg brewery, this major art and sculpture gallery centres on an impressive atrium, with palms, ferns and a pool. Key collections cover art from the ancient world, and French art of the 19th and 20th centuries, with sculptures by Rodin and Degas and paintings by Monet, Cézanne, Gauguin and many more. There's a more modest but representative selection of Danish art from the same period.

Dantes Plads 7. Tel: (033) 41 81 41. www.glyptoteket.dk. Open: Tue–Sun 11am–5pm. Admission charge (Sun free). Metro: Kongens Nytorv.

Rådhuspladsen (Town Hall Square)

Ringed by busy roads, the square is a gathering place enlivened by food stalls, markets and performers. To the right (west) of the handsome red-brick **Rådhuset** is a statue of Hans Christian Andersen, sculpted by H L Nielsen in 1961.

Rundetaarn has an observatory at the top

On the east side of the square is **H C Andersen Eventyrhuset** (Hans Christian Andersen's Wonderful World), which introduces Andersen's life and stories. However, if you're really interested in this great storyteller, try to make time to visit his birthplace in Odense, about 90 minutes away by train.

H C Andersen Eventyrhuset, Rådhuspladsen 57. Tel: (033) 32 31 31. www.topattractions.dk. Open: mid-Jun–Aug daily 10am–10pm; Sept–mid-Jun Sun–Thur 10am–6pm, Fri & Sat 10am–8pm. Admission charge. Metro: Kongens Nytorv.

Northeast from Rådhuspladsen runs pedestrianised **Strøget**, Copenhagen's main shopping street. To its north lies the Latin Quarter, full of bars, restaurants and offbeat shops.

Rundetaarn

The Round Tower offers a panorama of the city rooftops from 35m (115ft)

above the street, reached by a remarkable spiral stone ramp, which visiting royalty have sometimes ascended on horseback. The rest of us, less grand or just less idle, have to walk. The tower also houses the oldest functioning observatory in Europe – open during the dark winter months.

Købmagergade 52a. Tel: (033) 73 03 73. www.rundetaarn.dk. Open: late May–mid-Sept daily 10am–8pm; mid-Sept–May daily 10am–5pm. Admission charge. Metro: Nørreport.

Tivoli

Opened in 1843, Tivoli is one of the oldest leisure gardens in the world, and Denmark's most popular attraction. It has a lake, elaborate floral displays, bandstands, amusement rides traditional and modern, and more than three dozen food outlets, ranging from hotdog stands to gourmet restaurants and a fine brew-pub. The concert hall stages regular performances by international artists and has its own symphony orchestra. The same building houses a popular aquarium. *Tel: (033) 15 10 01. www.tivoli.dk. Open: Easter–mid-Jun & mid-Aug–Sept daily 11am–11pm; mid-Jun–mid-Aug Sun–Thur 11am–midnight, Fri & Sat 11am–12.30am; early–mid-Oct Sun–Thur 10am–10pm, Fri & Sat 10am–11pm; mid-Nov–Dec Mon–Fri 11am–9pm, Sat 10am–10pm, Sun 10am–9pm. Closed: mid-Sept–early Oct, mid-Oct–mid-Nov & Jan–Easter. Admission charge. Metro: Nørreport.*

The north of the city
Amalienborg
Amalienborg is an octagonal courtyard surrounded by four matched palaces; along with the nearby **Marmorkirken** (Marble Church), these represent the grand vision of Frederik V, whose equestrian effigy is at the centre.
Amalienborg Palace (the one on the southwest side) only became a royal residence when fire destroyed Christiansborg in 1794. It remains the Danish monarch's 'town house' and when the queen is in residence, the Changing of the Guard takes place at noon every day. **Amalienborgmuseet** includes private apartments and State rooms, with furnishings and decoration mostly from the 19th century, plus displays of jewellery and costumes. *Tel: (033) 12 21 86. www.amalienborgmuseet.dk. Open: May–Oct daily 10am–4pm; Nov–Apr Tue–Sun 11am–4pm. Admission charge. Metro: Kongens Nytorv.*

Statens Museum for Kunst

Kastellet
A short way north of Amalienborg, the five great fortified bastions of Kastellet are now grassed over and covered in flowers in spring. With its moat and surrounding parkland, it's one of the most peaceful parts of Copenhagen, though some of the 18th-century barracks buildings remain in military hands. The central street and ramparts are open during the daytime.

Kongens Have (King's Garden)
The King's Garden, laid out in 1606, is a favourite place for lunch breaks on a sunny day. On its northwest side is **Rosenborg Slot** (Rosenborg Castle). Enlarged from a royal summer house, by 1633 it looked as it does today, a tall red-brick structure in Dutch Renaissance style. It was a royal residence until 1710; today it is a repository for the royal collections of art and other treasures, including the Crown Jewels and other royal regalia. *Oster Volgade. Tel: (033) 15 32 86. www.rosenborgslot.dk. Open: Jun–Aug*

daily 10am–5pm; May, Sept & Oct daily 10am–4pm; Feb–Apr Tue–Fri 11am–4pm; Nov–Jan Tue–Fri 11am–2pm. Admission charge. Metro: Nørreport.

Kongens Nytorv (New Royal Square)

The New Royal Square is the focal point of Copenhagen's 'New Town', dating from the 17th and 18th centuries; it abuts the landward end of Nyhavn (*see p107*).

Statens Museum for Kunst (Danish National Gallery)

Denmark's National Gallery is the premier place to study the development of Danish art, and also has notable collections of European art from 1300 to 1800 – including French, Italian and, above all, Dutch and Flemish masters – and 20th-century art, too, including works by great artists such as Matisse, Modigliani and Picasso.
Sølvgade 48–50. Tel: (033) 74 84 94. www.smk.dk. Open: Tue & Thur–Sun 10am–5pm, Wed 10am–8pm. Admission charge for special exhibitions. Metro: Nørreport.

AROUND COPENHAGEN: HELSINGØR (ELSINORE), HILLERØD AND ROSKILDE

Two great attractions northwest of Copenhagen can easily be linked in a triangular excursion. Trains between Helsingør and Hillerød are roughly hourly, so check times carefully; the trains between Copenhagen and each place are more frequent.

Helsingør is a cruise port in its own right, but it's only 40 minutes by train from Copenhagen, along the 'Danish Riviera'. **Kronborg Slot** (Elsinore Castle) is the main draw, but it's a charming town with a fine cathedral. From the railway station it's a well-signed ten-minute walk to the castle, past a small harbour and a former warehouse area, which is now becoming an attractive arty quarter.

Denmark

Kronborg Slot, 'Hamlet's Castle', is a must for literature buffs

Kronborg Slot

Elsinore's role in Shakespeare's play has ensured that Kronborg Slot is renowned as 'Hamlet's Castle'. It is now a World Heritage Site, and externally it does largely date from Shakespeare's time, essentially built between 1574 and 1585, and restored following a major fire in 1629. Cross the outer moat and enter Kronværksporten, a 17th-century gate. The Kronværket area has several galleries, workshops and a café. Only after crossing the inner moat do you enter the castle proper, with its grand courtyard, opulent royal bedchambers, lavishly decorated chapel and the 62m (205ft) long ballroom.

Tel: (033) 92 63 00. www.ses.dk. Open: May–Sept daily 10.30am–5pm; Oct & Apr Tue–Sun 11am–4pm; Nov–Mar Tue–Sun 11am–3pm.
Admission charge.

Don't miss a walk to the point of the headland, overlooking the 4km (2½-mile) strait separating Denmark from Sweden. This underlines the strategic importance of the castle, which once collected dues from vessels navigating the strait. Today, the area is popular with sea-anglers, while ships of all kinds ply through the narrows, and a stream of ferries churns across to Helsingborg – a 25-minute crossing with unbeatable views of the castle.

Hillerød

Hillerød is a pleasant small town, with one great attraction: **Frederiksborg Slot**. Standing on islands in a small lake, it's arguably the most beautiful of Denmark's royal castles. A walk around the lake, taking in the parkland and formal gardens, takes at least half an hour; far better than rushing straight to the castle. Remains of the first castle, built by Frederik II, are completely overshadowed by Christian IV's 'new' castle, built between 1599 and 1622. A favoured royal residence for a century, it was badly damaged by fire in 1859 and, after restoration, became a national historical museum, with major collections of furniture and paintings.

Tel: (048) 26 04 39. www. frederiksborgmuseet.dk. Castle open: Apr–Oct daily 10am–5pm; Nov–Mar daily 11am–3pm. Admission charge. Park open: May–Aug daily 10am–9pm; Sept & Apr daily 10am–7pm; Oct & Mar daily 10am–5pm; Nov–Feb daily 10am–4pm. Free admission.

The enchanting Frederiksborg Slot

Roskilde

To the casual visitor, Roskilde might appear a pleasant but unexceptional

Denmark

HAMLET AT ELSINORE

We know little definite about Shakespeare's life, but it's almost certain that he never visited Denmark, and indeed probably never left England. *Hamlet* was written around 1600, when Kronborg Slot was one of Europe's great new castles: its renown certainly reached Shakespeare's London. It seems to have been no more than a conveniently fabulous setting for a story that may have derived in part from legends such as the tale of Prince Amleth, which appears in the medieval Danish history, *Gesta Danorum*. Intriguingly, in this legend, Amleth travels twice to England, but nothing connects him specifically to Helsingør. 'Elsinore' is merely Shakespeare's Anglicisation of Helsingør.

present cathedral was largely built between 1170 and 1280. Later additions are mostly in the form of side-chapels, the main ones housing the royal tombs. It is one of the great medieval churches of Europe, and one of the great brick churches of any age. As well as the many royal tombs (perhaps the most significant being that of the great Margarete I, in the centre of the choir), an outstanding treasure is the magnificent gilded altarpiece.
Tel: (046) 35 16 24. Open: Apr–Sept Mon–Sat 9am–5pm, Sun 12.30–5pm; Oct–Mar Tue–Sat 10am–4pm, Sun 12.30–4pm. Admission charge.

town, but there's a great deal more to it; it was Denmark's first capital, and it is home to two remarkable attractions, the great medieval **Domkirke** (Cathedral), a World Heritage Site, and **Vikingeskibsmuseet** (the Viking Ship Museum). Either place would be worth a trip in its own right; that the two lie so close together is a bonus. And all this is just an easy half-hour train journey from Copenhagen.

To reach the cathedral, bear right leaving the station, cross a small square, and join the main pedestrian shopping street. At its far end is the tourist office and, just to the right, the cathedral.

Roskilde Domkirke

The first church on this site was erected a thousand years ago for Harald Blåtand (Harald Bluetooth), who became the first of a long line of monarchs to be buried here. The

Vikingeskibsmuseet (Viking Ship Museum)

From the cathedral, it's a pleasant walk through parkland down to the fjord and the Vikingeskibsmuseet. It's no more
(Cont. on p118)

Roskilde Domkirke with its gilded altar

The Vikings

The people we know today as the Vikings had their homelands in present-day Denmark, the southern half of Sweden and coastal areas of Norway. The period referred to as the Viking Age, approximately AD 800–1050, marks a time of expansion for these peoples, but they did not appear out of nowhere, nor did they disappear at the end of that time; they are the principal ancestors of most of the modern people of the three Scandinavian countries.

The word 'Viking' itself may – and then again, may not – have meant

A Viking rune stone on show at Skansen, Stockholm

something like 'pirate' or 'raider'. It's true that this is the stereotypical modern view of the Vikings, especially in nations like the UK. They certainly showed a combative and sometimes ruthless side, with empire-building tendencies, but of course the majority of Vikings were not warriors at all but farmers, fishermen, artisans and traders.

The historical importance of the Viking era lies in their expansionism, which was due to the technological superiority of their ships over other vessels of the time (at least in Europe).

The great Viking voyages took them all over the Baltic and far inland on great rivers. They reached the Mediterranean, Black and Caspian Seas, and settled in numbers in northern and eastern England and in northern Scotland. Other pockets of Viking settlement were in present-day Latvia, Russia and most famously in northern France, where they mingled with native inhabitants and became known as Normans.

From Shetland they struck out into the open ocean, reaching the Faroes and then Iceland. Previously uninhabited, and relatively little affected by subsequent contact with other peoples, Iceland is the nation

A longship displayed at Vikingskipsmuseet, Oslo

where the influence of the Vikings is most strongly felt, and where most of the great Norse sagas were recorded. From Iceland, ships continued west, reaching southern Greenland and then, around AD 1000, Leifur Eiríksson landed somewhere he called Vinland. This is commonly identified with Newfoundland, in Canada, where archaeological evidence proves that there was a Viking settlement. Others believe that Vinland was further south, possibly in New England.

Viking sites

Key Viking sites for today's enquiring visitor include the Viking ship museums in Oslo and at Roskilde in Denmark, but a more rounded picture of Viking life may be gained at **Birka**, a World Heritage Site about 48km (30 miles) west of Stockholm, best reached from there by boat (allow a full day for the round trip and visit). A complete Viking town has been excavated here; a fascinating museum makes sense of the remains, and in high season there are demonstrations and re-enactments.

Birka island, Lake Mälar. Tel: (085) 605 1445. www.raa.se. Open: May–early Sept daily 10am–5pm. Note that ferry services to Birka island only run in summer months.

than 800m (½ mile) – ignore one sign that claims it's 1.2km (¾ mile). In the Viking period Roskilde was an important trading centre, and as such ran the risk of attack. Ships were sunk to blockade two of the three navigable channels, and when archaeologists began to investigate them in the 1960s they identified the remains of five vessels. Excavation was a painstaking task, taking several years, but it seems almost hasty compared to the 25 years it took to conserve the remains and piece together the five ships, all of which can now be seen in the purpose-built museum, bathed in the cool northern light from the fjord. Three are cargo vessels, two are warships. The larger of these, which had a crew of 80, was built in Dublin around 1042 (this is known from analysis of the growth rings in the oak timbers).

Replicas of all five ships have been built in the yard adjacent to the museum, using authentic tools and techniques as far as possible. This process has also yielded much information about Viking technology and has helped our understanding of their success as seafarers. The replicas can usually be seen at the dock, and sometimes sailing on the fjord. The large warship has been much further afield, making a successful voyage to Dublin in 2007 and returning in 2008. *Tel: (045) 46 30 02 00. www.vikingeskibsmuseet.dk. Open: daily 9am–5pm. Admission charge.*

ÅRHUS

Denmark's second city, Århus is on the east coast of Jutland, the Danish mainland. Originating in Viking times, the city became a major port in the 17th century and grew strongly with industrialisation in the 19th. There's a fine **Domkirke** (Cathedral), a **Viking Museum** in the unlikely setting of a bank basement, and many more museums and galleries, particularly in the district north of the cathedral, known as the Latin Quarter. Today, Århus thrives on trade and modern high-tech industries; with a youthful population and a high proportion of students, it's a leading cultural centre and also boasts one of the world's best open-air museums.

Lovers of art and architecture alike will make a beeline for **Århus Kunstmuseum** (ARoS), a startling 43m (141ft) high cuboid building opened in 2004. A 'Museum Street', freely open to the public, curves through the middle of the structure. The main galleries display mostly Danish art, from the 'Golden Age' to the contemporary cutting edge.

The Århus Kunstmuseum

Denmark

Den Gamle By recreates 'old' Denmark

Aros Allé 2. Tel: (045) 87 30 66 00.
www.aros.dk. Open: Tue & Thur–Sun
10am–5pm, Wed 10am–10pm.
Admission charge.

Den Gamle By

It simply means the 'Old Town', but this
is not some surviving quarter of old
Århus. It is a purpose-built open-air
museum, with buildings from all over
Denmark, dating from the 17th to the
19th centuries, and reassembled along
the river. For most of the year it's full of
costumed role-players, embodying the
phrase 'living history'. You can visit four
complete homes, three working
kitchens, a bakery, a bookshop, an
ironmonger's and much more. Special
exhibitions and events are regularly
staged, with the Christmas Market
being very popular.
Viborgvej. Tel: (045) 86 12 31 88.
www.dengamleby.dk. Open: Jan–mid-
Feb daily 11am–3pm; mid-Feb–Mar
daily 10am–4pm; Apr–late Jun & early
Sept–mid-Nov daily 10am–5pm; late

Jun–early Sept daily 9am–6pm; mid-
Nov–late Dec Mon–Fri 9am–7pm,
Sat–Sun 10am–7pm. Admission charge.

BORNHOLM

Bornholm lies around 150km (90
miles) east of Copenhagen, though
much closer to Sweden. It has ferry
links with Ystad (Sweden), Sassnitz in
Germany and Świnoujście in Poland.
It's hardly surprising that it has
changed hands many times, leaving a
rich and varied historical legacy. The
island is equally rich geologically, with
granite in the north more than a billion
years old and much younger sandstone
in the south. The landscape, with its
cliffs, waterfalls, serene forests, rolling
fields and glorious beaches, has been
called 'Scandinavia in a nutshell'.
Hyperbole, perhaps, but pardonable.

Rønne

Almost 700 years old, Rønne is the main
town and cruise port. In the older areas
many half-timbered houses survive, but
interspersed with brick homes known as
'bomb houses'. These replaced houses
destroyed by Russian bombing in 1945.
Rønne has many museums, galleries,
and the oldest theatre in Denmark.

Bornholm has several medieval
round churches; heavily fortified, they
doubled as refuges when raiders
appeared. About 20km (12½ miles)
east of Rønne, **Østerlars Kirke**, dated to
c. 1150, is the largest and best known.
Open: all year. Small admission charge
in summer.

Norway

Norway has long been a magnet for cruises, particularly to the great western fjords. The scenery of the south is less grandiose but scarcely less beautiful, and Oslo is a graceful, cosmopolitan and easy-going city. Norway also enjoys one of the highest standards of living in the world but, it must be said, eating and drinking can be very expensive.

OSLO

Oslo has a lot going for it, notably its gorgeous natural setting. Its inhabitants value this highly and strive to keep development sympathetic. Oslo is also a city of peace; home to the Nobel Peace Prize; one of the world's safest cities to visit – and also one where the roar of traffic is blessedly muted, thanks to strategic tunnels and excellent public transport. It's a vibrant centre of arts and culture, with some unique and fascinating museums.

Approaches

Oslo stands at the head of Oslofjord, 80km (50 miles) from open sea. Glaciated skerries line the outer approaches, then rolling fields and woods. Further on, the fjord narrows dramatically and the scenery steepens; the course twists into the lake-like inner reach, with the city cradled by hills.

The cruise terminal is ideally placed, below the fortress of Akershus Fastning, with the towers of Rådhuset (City Hall)

just ahead and the new complex of Aker Brygge, crammed with shops and restaurants, across the inner harbour. Buses, trams and the Bygdøy ferry are three minutes' walk away, the metro a fraction further.

The city centre

Rådhusplassen, between the harbour and the Rådhuset, is an exhilarating space, often enlivened by street performers. Early in the day (7–8am), fresh fish are sold straight off the boat. Head inland, past Rådhuset, to a pleasant park beside Karl Johans Gate. West from here is the Royal Palace and the surrounding Slottsparken, while further east Karl Johans Gate is pedestrianised and makes another lively focus for street life.

Operaen (Opera House)

Oslo's sparkling new Opera House (opened April 2008) instantly became a favourite gathering place on sunny days; walk up the great limestone ramps

The approach to Oslo by sea, with the Rådhuset dominating the skyline

to the roof to discover why. It isn't ideally placed for the best views, but that hardly matters. Wander into the foyer too; it's equally striking. And all free.
Kirsten Flagstads Plass 1.
Tel (047) 21 42 21 00. www.operaen.no.
Metro: Jernbanetorget.

North and west of the centre
Holmenkollen
Holmenkollen's ski-jump tower, with its amazing views over the city 400m (1,300ft) below, is Oslo's leading attraction. The old tower was demolished in 2008 and its replacement opened in 2010, ready to host the World Championships in 2011. The 60m-high tower is also home to the world's oldest museum of skiing.
Tel: (047) 91 67 19 47.
www.skiforeningen.no. Open: Jun–Sept daily 10am–4pm; Oct–Apr Mon–Fri 10am–3pm, Sat–Sun 10am–4pm.
Admission charge. Metro: Holmenkollen.

Vigelandsparken
There are many sculpture parks in Europe, but none quite like this. It was the life's work of sculptor Gustav Vigeland (1869–1943). Two hundred and twelve pieces are arrayed around a park also designed by Vigeland, forming an integrated statement in celebration of the human body and indeed humanity itself – loving, laughing, leaping – that fuses exuberance and tenderness.

The park also houses the Vigeland Museum, telling the story of the man and his works (closed for renovation until May 2011).
2km (1¼ miles) northwest of the city. Tram 12 or bus to Vigelandsparken. Open: daily 24 hrs.
Vigeland Museum. Tel: (047) 23 49 37 00. www.vigeland.museum.no. Open: Jun– Aug Tue–Sun 11am–5pm; Sept–May Tue–Sun noon–4pm. Admission charge (Apr–Sept only).

Tour: Around Bygdøy by bike

As well as a great way to reach Bygdøy and its museums, this ride reveals another side of Oslo, with peaceful woods, farms and beaches. The route is flexible, as you can opt to return from Bygdøy by ferry or, if you're using a City Bike (see p140), you can leave it at the stand by the Folkemuseum.

Start from **Rådhusplassen** (*see p120*); there's a City Bike stand near the tram stop on the west side. Follow the tram tracks towards Aker Brygge (the waterfront) and then swing right and up slightly. Approaching an overpass,

turn left onto a signed cycle track. Follow this, passing the 'back' of Aker Brygge, then a container port and the Color Line ferry terminal.

Continue for another 2km (1¼ miles) alongside a marina, with the E18

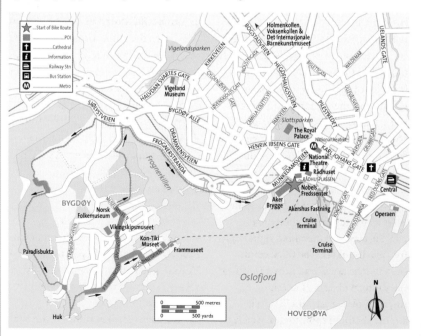

The *Fram* took Amundsen to the South Pole

tarmac lane following signs for Hokødden and then Huk badsplass. Drop down steeply and bear right, across a bus turning circle, into park-like greenery. Go right at the first fork and ride out to the headland of Huk, with its rocky outcrops, sandy beach and (possibly welcome) café.

Backtrack about 100m (110yds) then fork right before a volleyball court. At a T-junction go right; tarmac turns to gravel, then tarmac resumes as houses appear. Turn right at a crossroads on Konsul Schelderups vei then go left on P T Mallingsvei. Follow this quiet residential street to a junction with Bygdøynesveien (on the right), usually marked by a sudden increase in traffic.

Bygdøynesveien leads to the *Fram* and *Kon-Tiki* Museums (*see p124*): you could visit these now and backtrack to this point, but a better plan (especially with a City Bike) is to continue straight ahead on Langviksvei. You soon pass **Vikingskipsmuseet** (*see p125*) and it's another 400m (¼ mile) to the **Norsk Folkemuseum** (*see p125*). You can leave City Bikes at the stand here; it's then possible to get the bus down to *Fram/Kon-Tiki*, and from there take the ferry back.

To ride all the way back, go on a short way past the Folkemuseum, then bear right on a signed cycle track. Keep straight on at junctions until you rejoin the busier road. Turn right and skim down to the wooden hut at the roundabout, then retrace from here.

motorway (Frognerstranda) beyond the hedge on the other side. At the end of the inlet and marina, by a wooden hut, is a junction.

Fork right, dipping under the Bygdøy road. Go past a sports ground. Roughly opposite a footbridge, turn left then fork right (sign for Bygdøy sjøbad). Climb a bit then continue on a gravel track. Follow this, keeping straight ahead at any junctions, now in rural surroundings. The path joins a dirt road, which acquires tarmac above a small harbour and bathing area.

Follow the tarmac road to the left. After a rise, fork right through a parking area and then keep right (signs for Paradisbukta). The track climbs, then swings down and runs parallel to the shore, with lots of tempting stopping places. At Paradisbukta, another bathing spot, continue along a

Bygdøy

The promontory of Bygdøy has an exceptional clutch of museums. An ideal way to arrive is by ferry from Rådhusplassen (*Apr–Oct*); another is by bike (*see pp122–3*). Bus No 30 also serves Bygdøy.

Frammuseet (*Fram* Museum)

The *Fram* is reckoned to be the strongest wooden ship ever built; she is unquestionably the most famous ship in the history of Polar exploration. In 1893–6 she carried Nansen's expedition to a 'farthest north' point, which was unbeaten by a surface vessel for over a century; in 1910–11 she took Amundsen's expedition to Antarctica for their successful journey to the South Pole. Visitors can go aboard, view the cramped cabins and visit the saloon, complete with piano and wind-up gramophone.

This ship is the *Gjøa*, in which Amundsen completed the Northwest Passage

FRIDTJOF NANSEN

Fridtjof Nansen (1861–1930) was one of those rare individuals who achieved greatness in several fields. On the *Fram*'s first voyage, having reached 84°4′ North, it became clear that the ship would not be carried by the ice to the Pole, so with Hjalmar Johansen, Nansen set out on skis, reaching a new 'farthest north' of 86°14′. Nansen subsequently achieved distinction in the fields of both oceanography and zoology. After World War I he worked for the League of Nations, striving to help refugees and famine victims. This work earned him the Nobel Peace Prize in 1922.

Bygdøynesveien 36. Tel: (047) 23 28 29 50. www.fram.museum.no. Open: Jun–Aug daily 9am–6pm; May & Sept daily 10am–5pm; Oct, Mar & Apr daily 10am–4pm; Nov–Feb Mon–Fri 10am–3pm, Sat & Sun 10am–4pm. Admission charge.

Kon-Tiki Museet (*Kon-Tiki* Museum)

Kon-Tiki recalls another tale of audacity just the right side of madness. In this tiny raft Thor Heyerdahl and five companions sailed from Peru to Polynesia, demonstrating that ancient mariners could have voyaged much farther than previously believed. The museum also houses the papyrus boat *Ra II*, in which Heyerdahl and a multinational crew crossed the Atlantic in 1970.
Bygdøynesveien 36. Tel: (047) 23 08 67 67. www.kon-tiki.no. Open: Jun–Aug daily 9.30am–5.30pm; Apr, May & Sept daily 10am–5pm; Mar & Oct daily 10am–4pm; Nov–Feb daily 10.30am–3.30pm. Admission charge.

Shop for traditional products at the Norsk Folkemuseum

Norsk Folkemuseum
(Norwegian Folk Museum)

The Norwegian Folk Museum features meticulously reconstructed farms and villages from around the country; many interiors are open to view, with guardians in appropriate costume to explain and demonstrate. Highlights include the 800-year-old Stave Church, dark and mysterious inside. An urban section includes a lovely manor house, and a shop with products you can buy (at 21st-century prices, alas!).

Museumsveien 10. Tel: (047) 22 12 37 00. www.norskfolkemuseum.no. Open: mid-May–mid-Sept daily 10am–6pm; mid-Sept–mid-May Mon–Fri 11am–3pm, Sat & Sun 11am–4pm. Admission charge.

Vikingskipsmuseet
(Viking Ship Museum)

A purpose-built building houses three Viking ships, two of them probably the best preserved ever found. All three were ultimately used in burials, and grave-goods have yielded much information about Viking life. The decorated Oseberg ship (built *c.* AD 815–20) is superficially the most impressive, but the Gokstad ship (*c.* 890) is larger and a true seagoing vessel. Associated finds include fabrics, jewellery and a rare Viking carriage.

Huk Aveny 35. Tel: (047) 22 13 52 80. www.ukm.uio.no. Open: May–Sept 9am–6pm; Oct–Apr 10am–4pm. Admission charge.

When to go

If you opt for a regular cruise, then your choice is limited by the operating season, typically May to September. The peak holiday season in most of the Baltic countries runs from midsummer (23–24 June) to the middle or end of August. It makes less difference in the major cities, but in smaller places some attractions are only open during this period, and many have more limited opening hours for the rest of the year.

The 'shoulder' seasons (May and much of June and September) are good times to visit, and cruise prices may well be somewhat lower. Between October and April you will have to look for other options, such as a 'DIY cruise' (*see pp24–5*); most of the scheduled ferry

Winter in Helsinki can be cold, but magical

services run throughout the year. This means that the main ports aren't full of other cruise passengers, and accommodation prices may be a bit lower. In the cities, at least, all the main attractions remain open.

Naturally the weather is a major consideration, and the northerly latitudes of the Baltic do deter some people. Copenhagen, southernmost of the major cities, stands at 55°41' N. For comparison, this is similar to Glasgow and well to the north of all Canada's major cities. Helsinki, the northernmost of the main Baltic ports, is at 60°11' N. Winters *are* cold, but maritime influences mean they are nowhere near as severe as they can be in the Midwest or Canada's Prairie provinces. Summers are usually pleasantly warm but rarely uncomfortably hot.

What is very noticeable is the fluctuation in the length of the day. Even Helsinki is more than six degrees south of the Arctic Circle, so there is no

Spring on the shores of the Peter and Paul Fortress, St Petersburg

midnight sun in summer or 24-hour darkness in winter. Still, at midsummer the sun only dips below the horizon for a few hours and it never gets really dark, producing the famed 'white nights'. St Petersburg, which is only a fraction further south, also sets great store by these. Stockholm and Oslo also stand north of 59°.

To visit any of these cities in high summer can be almost disorienting at first, with the sun apparently stubbornly refusing to set. Many find it hard to sleep and it sometimes seems as if the locals just don't bother: probably they catch up in the winter. This helps to explain the great significance of midsummer (*see Festivals p18*) in most of the Baltic lands; on the night of 23 June staying up all night is practically *de rigueur*. It stands to

geographical reason that the ultimate place to experience midsummer festivities, at least within the compass of this book, is Helsinki.

Of course, the converse of this is that at midwinter the hours of daylight are short. However, against that there's a realistic chance, even today, of a 'white Christmas', with snow helping make the best of what light there is. Alternatively, visiting in February or early March means there's plenty of daylight and an even better chance of snow on the ground. Cross-country skiing is widely practised and Oslo has real Alpine skiing within the city limits.

It all depends on your tastes, of course, but there's no monsoon or hurricane season; in other words, there's no really bad time of year to come to the Baltic.

Getting around

For most readers, this is all taken care of by the cruise ship, but not for DIY cruisers. There are lots of scheduled ferries, and the possible permutations of route are legion – but then planning can be half the fun! See below for some suggestions.

Local transport

Depending on your package, the cruise company may be taking care of it all. If the cruise terminal isn't handy to the city, there's usually a shuttle bus, and/or you may have opted for organised excursions. If you're doing your own thing, however, be reassured that all the larger cities have comprehensive public transport networks.

City passes

If you plan on doing sightseeing on your own in the main cities, it's worth investigating city passes/cards – the Oslo Pass, Turku Card and so on. For a one-off payment, these give free travel on city transport and free entry to most museums and attractions. Additional benefits may include discounts at shops and restaurants. The cost–benefit equation depends on how long you are staying and how much you plan to see, but typically a 24-hour card will pay for itself if you visit three museums and take a few rides on public transport.

Public transport

A city pass will usually come with a handy booklet giving hints on using public transport and probably including network maps. If you're making the odd journey without a pass, here are a few hints.

On trams and buses it's often possible to pay the driver, but you'll usually also find a newsstand next to most stops where you can buy tickets in advance. Usually you have to validate your ticket when you board – watch how the locals do it. For metros and trains, buy tickets in advance. Stations usually have ticket machines, often with instructions in English. On buses, trams and metro it's almost universal that you pay one price per journey, regardless of length.

St Petersburg's legendary metro has ticket machines but hardly anyone uses them. Join the queue at the ticket window instead. The price of a single ticket is displayed at every window: just hand over the money, or the next

Trams are a good way to get around Rīga – copy what the locals do with their tickets

round sum, and you'll get change and a token that works the turnstile.

Scheduled ferry services

Finnlines (*www.finnlines.fi*) has several routes of interest, e.g. Gdynia–Helsinki. For the adventurous, **TransRussiaExpress** (*www.tre.de*) has weekly sailings (passenger accommodation on a cargo vessel) to St Petersburg from Lübeck and Sassnitz.

Lisco (*www.dfdslisco.com*), now part of DFDS, serves, among others, Klaipėda–Karlshamn (Sweden) and Rīga–Lübeck.

Polferries (*www.polferries.pl*) has routes including Gdańsk–Nynäshamn.

Scandlines (*www.scandlines.lt*) sails from Ventspils (Lithuania) to Travemünde and to Nynäshamn (on Stockholm's local train network).

Stena Line (*www.stenaline.com*) has routes such as Frederikshavn (Denmark)–Oslo and Gdynia–Karlskrona (Sweden).

Tallink ferries (*www.tallinksilja.com*) sails under Tallink and Silja names between, for instance, Stockholm and Rīga and Rostock and Helsinki. They, and others, also offer crossings between Tallinn and Helsinki – the fastest take just 90 minutes.

Viking Line (*www.vikingline.fi*) (as well as Tallink-Silja) covers the magical Stockholm–Mariehamn–Turku route, and also reaches Helsinki and Tallinn.

Useful overview sites include *www.directferries.co.uk*, *www.aferry.to* and *www.ferrysavers.co.uk*

Food and drink

Diverse cultural traditions as well as variations in soil and climate yield a wide range of food and drink across the region, but there are some common elements. One of these is seasonality. Chefs and restaurants across the world have been rediscovering the importance of seasonal produce, and in the Baltic seasons are really pronounced. Most cruise travellers will be visiting the region in summer, a time of special abundance when fresh local food is particularly celebrated.

Seafood, naturally, is important. The low salinity of the Baltic (lower still in the Gulf of Finland) blurs the usual distinction between saltwater and freshwater species. A common, and initially puzzling, occurrence on menus is 'pike-perch', as pike and perch are quite different fish. The name refers to fish of the genus *Sander*, which does look vaguely like a pike. Anyway, it's delicious.

Long harsh winters promote use of preserved and stored foods, such as pickles (notably sauerkraut), dried mushrooms, smoked meat and sausages. Finland and Sweden, particularly, still rely on cold-tolerant animals, mainly reindeer. Reindeer meat is low in cholesterol and, if properly prepared, high in flavour.

'Medieval' restaurants abound, but vary widely in their level of authenticity. If there are potatoes (or, God forbid, chips!) on the menu, it's not medieval. The spud only arrived in Europe in the late 16th century, and did not reach the Baltic until the 17th. As the same applies to tobacco, patrons clearly should not smoke either! While other root vegetables were known, the main source of carbohydrate in the Middle Ages was usually bread.

Today, the potato is firmly established: Russia is the world's second largest producer after China. However, bread remains a staple, and comes in many forms. Rye bread is common, whether it's dense German pumpernickel (baked for 16–24 hours), a light Russian loaf with treacly overtones, or the bewildering variety found in Finnish bakeries, from crackly crispbreads to soft, fragrant, ring-shaped loaves.

From the Hanseatic era onwards, German influence has been strong, especially in the southern half of the Baltic. Sweden took its turn as the dominant power before the rise of Russia, with its long rule over Finland and the Baltic States. All have left their culinary mark.

Blood sausage, a local delicacy in Rīga

Common Russian dishes include robust soups like *schi* (based on cabbage) and meaty *solyanka*. The best-known soup is *borscht*, usually based on beetroot and garnished with sour cream; it's also common in Poland (*barszcz*) and Lithuania (*barščiai*). *Shashlik* is meat grilled on a skewer and *blini* are small pancakes that can have sweet or savoury fillings. *Pirogi* are small dumplings, baked or boiled (and sometimes fried), filled with meat, vegetables, cheese or fruit. In Poland they are called *pierogi*, and are also common in Latvia (*pīrāgi*) and Lithuania.

The Scandinavian tradition places greater emphasis on seafood. Herring (fresh or pickled) is a staple; salmon (*lax*) is another. *Gravad lax* is dill-marinated salmon. Lobster (*hummer*) also goes down well. Again, bread is central and underpins a dazzling variety of open sandwiches (Swedish: *smörgås*; Norwegian: *smørbrød*; Danish: *smørrebrød*; Finnish: *volleipä*). For dessert, look out for luscious cloudberries from Lapland.

In German tradition, meat, especially pork, is central to the menu. It's usually stewed or pot-roasted. Preserved meats like hams and salamis are very common, and of course Germany produces a vast variety of sausages (*Wurst*). Over most of Germany, fish naturally means freshwater fish like trout, pike, perch and carp, but on the north coast these are joined by sea-fish, including that Baltic speciality, the herring. Noodles are often served instead of potatoes.

Today, there's not a port around the Baltic where you'll have trouble finding pizza or a burger. Italian, Indian and Chinese restaurants are everywhere, joined by a new Japanese wave, especially in Russia and the Baltics. Germany has numerous Turkish restaurants, while Russia's imperial past means there are many Ukrainian, Armenian, Uzbek and other eateries. Generally, however, restaurant listings in the book are biased towards indigenous cuisine. Pizza is great but you can get it anywhere, which you can't say about Latvian grey peas with bacon.

Vegetarians

The traditional, cold-climate, meat-heavy Baltic diet is not exactly conducive to vegetarianism. In Germany and the Nordic countries, cosmopolitan influences mean most restaurants offer vegetarian options, but this is less certain elsewhere. However, there's usually a way. For example, *pirogi* or *blini* with cheese provide a local and economical alternative to yet another mushroom pizza.

Drink

The Baltic climate favours grain not grapes, and beer is the traditional drink. (Germany is a noted wine producer, but almost all comes from much further south.) Denmark and Germany produce global beer brands, and pilsner-style lagers are available everywhere. However, there are many more distinctive and interesting brews to be found, mostly through microbreweries and brew-pubs, of which, fortunately, numbers are growing steadily.

Baltic porter is usually high in alcohol, slightly sweet and often with a finish reminiscent of dark chocolate (cynics say 'cough medicine'). Around the region, other specialist beers include dark lagers (these are popular in Sweden around Christmas, when they're called *Julöl*), beers with herb or spice flavourings (often found in medieval-themed restaurants) and beers produced wholly or partly from other grains such as wheat, oats or rye. Beers made with honey are popular in Latvia and, even more so, in Lithuania.

Germany produces a wide variety of beer types. The *Reinheitsgebot* (purity law) was repealed in 1987, but most German breweries still observe the standard, although added yeast is now commonplace. Originally only barley, hops and water could be used, relying on natural yeast in the atmosphere to promote fermentation. Germany also produces many 'wheat' beers (most use a mix of wheat and barley); *Hefeweizen* (literally yeast-wheat) is a bottle-conditioned live beer.

Along with beer, there's a strong spirit-drinking tradition. In Scandinavia this usually means *akvavit*; the name comes from the Latin *aqua vitae*, or water of life, so in a sense it's synonymous with whisky (Gaelic *uisge-beatha*). *Akvavit* may be distilled from potatoes or from grain. Various flavourings are added, caraway being perhaps the commonest, and it is often aged in oak casks, acquiring an amber hue. The German equivalent is *Schnaps*, distilled from fruit, sometimes with additional flavourings.

From Poland to Russia, and on to Finland, vodka is the dominant spirit, usually clear but sometimes with added flavourings. Traditionally vodka is taken neat, in small doses knocked back in one hit. Repeated, sometimes competitive, toasts can lead the unwary to consume far more than they are prepared for.

A café in Raekoja plats, Tallinn

Food and drink

Entertainment

On a typical cruise, entertainment is largely catered for on board, and with port calls often limited to daylight hours, nightlife on shore may be barely relevant. Of course, bars and pubs usually serve at lunchtime, too. Otherwise, nightlife and entertainment are mostly mentioned in the main ports, where longer stays are more likely. Those travelling independently will usually have little difficulty finding congenial drinking spots even in the smaller ports.

There's something a bit different about nightlife in the Baltic, certainly in summer. The 'white nights' seem to encourage everyone to stay up late. There's something special about sipping a beer in the open air and watching the sun set – at midnight.

All the major cities have English-language listings papers that will keep you abreast of what's going on. In summer, free performances, from street-theatre to large-scale open-air concerts, are widespread.

Music

All the main cities have vibrant music scenes.

Classical music

Apart from the capitals, some of the other cities also have notable orchestras, nowhere more so than Göteborg. *Göteborgs Symfoniker* is the national orchestra of Sweden and its music director, Gustavo Dudamel, is now an established star on the world stage.

Folk music

Nowhere is folk music more relevant or more poignant than in the Baltic States (*see The Singing Revolutions, pp84–5*). The great Song Festivals take place only once every five years, but smaller performances happen regularly. There's usually music in the air at the open-air museums in Tallinn and Rīga (and, for that matter, at Seurasaari in Helsinki and Skansen in Stockholm).

Jazz

Jazz is very popular throughout the region, as the number of festivals testifies. Our listings note some of the best jazz clubs; check local listings papers as there will be many more, including open-air concerts.

Opera

Göteborg, Copenhagen and Oslo all have magnificent new opera houses, with state-of-the-art acoustics. They are used for concert performances and usually for ballet as well as opera.

Medieval musicians perform in Vanalinn, Tallinn

Helsinki's opera house is also relatively new. St Petersburg is home to the legendary Mariinsky (formerly Kirov) Opera and Ballet.

Rock and pop

Every variety of popular music is represented in the region. Heavy metal is very popular (surely only Finland could win Eurovision with a heavy metal number!) and open-air festivals proliferate in the summer.

Theatre

Theatre is strong in the Baltic, but of course performances are normally in the local language. Check the local listings papers for the exceptions.

Dance

Dance is popular, in one form or another, throughout the region. The dinner-dance is still a social mainstay in Finland in particular (*tanssiravintola* means dance-restaurant). It's also reckoned that the tango is more popular in Finland than anywhere else, possibly even including Argentina. Again, a visit to the main open-air museums, especially in high season, often offers a chance of seeing folk dancing.

Shopping

The Baltic for bargains? It depends. Nowhere in the region will you find a camera or mp3 player at half the London price (unless it's a fake). Shopping here is less about finding ultimate bargains and more about items that stand out either because of high quality and great design or because they are different from what you can get at home. Or even both. Obvious examples of the first category include distinctive art, crafts and so on. The second category includes Baltic amber, Russian nesting dolls and icons.

Moving on to a different country every day or two leaves cruise travellers with a particular headache. If you see something you like in Stockholm, how do you know you won't see it cheaper in Helsinki, or see something similar but even more appealing in Tallinn? But if you pass now, will you get another chance? There is no simple answer to this conundrum. Fluctuating exchange rates make it still more fiendish. But it's worth offering some words of advice.

First, if you see something you absolutely must have – *now*, go and have a cup of coffee. *Then*, if you're still absolutely sure you want it, buy it: finding it cheaper elsewhere will be the lesser of two evils.

Second, major global or European brands are available in all the main cities. In which case, *in general*, Scandinavia is probably the most expensive, Germany, Finland and Russia somewhat cheaper; Poland and the Baltic republics are the cheapest.

Always check prices carefully against the current exchange rate and compare against what you'd get in a January sale back home. All the main cities have sophisticated, well-stocked arcades and department stores. For instance, Helsinki's great department store, Stockmann, now has branches in St Petersburg, Tallinn and Rīga.

Scandinavia in general, and Norway in particular, has an unenviable reputation for being expensive. It's true that the cost of a half-decent meal or a pint of beer in Oslo can be shocking, but this does not apply equally to other commodities. It can, for instance, be a good place to shop for outdoor and winter clothing – let's face it, the Nordic nations know something about living and playing in extreme conditions!

Opening hours

Opening hours vary widely, and in tourist areas are usually extended during the summer season. Many places don't open until 10am, but then stay open till

7pm or 8pm, if not longer. Lunchtime closing is relatively uncommon.

Tax-free shopping

In all the Baltic nations, except Russia, 'tax-free shopping' signs are widely displayed. The scheme allows citizens of non-EU countries to recoup Value-Added Tax (VAT), which may amount to as much as 20 per cent of the purchase price (a minimum purchase applies). Ask for a Global Refund Cheque when making the purchase and present it when leaving the country to claim the refund – this is often possible at cruise terminals. Global Refund Offices can directly credit your account using your credit card. For more detail see *www.globalrefund.com*

AMBER – AN ORGANIC GEM

Amber is found in many parts of the world but the two main areas are the Dominican Republic and the Baltic. Amber is formed from fossilised tree-resin, originating about 40–60 million years ago. Classically its colour is – well – amber, but it can range from a darker brown to a cloudy white. 'Inclusions' such as insects preserved in the amber enhance its value (if genuine). Amber occurs widely around Baltic coasts, but the biggest deposits are in Russia's Kaliningrad Oblast and the neighbouring coasts of Poland, Lithuania and Latvia.

Amber

Amber is *the* Baltic product. It's usually worked into jewellery, but you can find other, and larger, items too. As prime source areas, the best places to shop for

You can pick up amber in most countries in this region, whether the usual orange colour or the equally beautiful green or yellow varieties

amber products are Klaipėda, Rīga and Gdańsk. In Rīga, street stalls congregate around Līvu laukums and behind St Peter's Church, while there are several smart shops in the Jēkaba Kazarmas (Jacob's Barracks) on Torna iela. There's also an Amber Museum in Konventa Seta. In Gdańsk, there are many amber workshops in Główne Miasto and artists set up stalls along ulica Mariacka. Gdánsk now has a dedicated Amber Museum (*Fore Gate Complex at the end of ul Długa. Tel: (058) 301 47 33. www.mhmg.gda.pl. Open: mid-Jun–mid-Sept Tue–Sat 10am–6pm, Sun 11am–6pm, Mon 11am–3pm; mid-Sept–mid-Jun Wed–Sat 10am–4pm, Sun 11am–4pm, Tue 11am–3pm*).

If your cruise doesn't visit any of these cities, Tallinn is probably the next best bet. Amber is readily available in Copenhagen, Stockholm and St Petersburg, but prices are somewhat higher.

DESIGN

The Nordic nations have a unique importance in the world of design. Quite why this should be is hard to fathom. Perhaps it derives from their great traditions of working in wood, or perhaps long dark winters focus the mind on the fittings and furnishings of the home. Today, Scandinavian design is everywhere, not least in IKEA furniture stores, now in almost 40 countries. Ironically the company is now Dutch-owned, but the main manufacturing and design centres are still based in Sweden, and individual designers are named for each piece of furniture.

Art Nouveau

Art Nouveau was not just an architectural style but found expression in interior design and the decorative arts. Not surprisingly, Rīga is the prime place to look for Art Nouveau-influenced products. Another area that could yield rich pickings is Helsinki's Design District (*see below*), where many antique shops can be found.

Fashion and design

In all the main cities, global designer names are concentrated on the main shopping streets and malls, from Strøget in Copenhagen to Nevskiy prospekt in St Petersburg. More individual and interesting designers congregate slightly off these axes; for example, in Copenhagen, try the Latin Quarter, north of Strøget in the vicinity of Rundetaarn (*see p111*). For handmade and craft products, open-air markets are often a good bet, like Kauppatori in Helsinki.

There's no doubt that the Nordic countries have a special affinity for design of all kinds, and Helsinki has its own Design District, centred south and west of the west end of Esplanade Park; the greatest concentration of designer outlets (including clothing, ceramics, jewellery and furniture) are on Uudenmaankatu, Annankatu and Erottankatu. Of course, there's plenty of talent at work elsewhere and prices may be lower in Tallinn or Rīga.

The iconic Russian doll comes in many versions, including world leaders and superheroes!

Sport and leisure

One of the questionable pleasures of cruising is the tendency to eat too much and exercise too little. Cruise ships do have exercise facilities – gyms, swimming pools, even climbing walls – but in the Baltic, where sea passages are mostly short and nocturnal, these tend to be underused. During daylight hours, with so much to see, exercise also tends to be sidelined. Still, fresh air and exercise promote both better sleep and a healthier appetite. Or maybe just make us less guilty about enjoying those fabulous meals.

An obvious answer is to kill two birds with one stone, and exercise while seeing the city, by walking, cycling or even, in some cases, kayaking.

Walking

This requires nothing more than suitable footwear and a map. Our suggested walking tours for some of the larger cities are a starting point. In smaller ports it's even easier to get around on foot. Several of the cities lend themselves to longer hikes too. Oslo is ideal and Holmenkollen is one good base. Backed by green hills, Gdynia is another good place for hiking. In Finland and Sweden 'Every Man's Right' gives you a legal right to walk just about anywhere.

Cycling

Cycling may burn no more calories than walking, but lets you cover a lot more distance. Most of the featured cities are very bike-friendly, with St Petersburg being the obvious exception: cycling amid its brawling traffic is only for the experienced.

Of course, you need a bike. Some cruise companies may have a few bikes for loan, and the more often they're asked, the more likely they are to provide them in future. If you're travelling independently, it's common for hotels to have bikes for guests' use – nowhere more so than in bike heaven, Copenhagen. Four of the cities have a

CITY BIKES

Copenhagen, Stockholm, Helsinki and Oslo all operate City Bike schemes, making hundreds of bikes available for general use throughout the summer months (May–November, if not longer). Bikes may be borrowed from one stand and returned to a different location, giving great flexibility. In Helsinki and Copenhagen, you just drop a coin into a slot as a token deposit. In Oslo and Stockholm, you should first buy a 'smart card' from a tourist information centre. In 2010 these cost 80NOK for a 1-day card in Oslo and 125SEK for a 3-day card in Stockholm.

The smooth waters of the Stockholm Archipelago offer perfect conditions for kayaking

public bike scheme (*see box*). If none of these help you, ask at a tourist information point about bike hire.

Quiet islands like Åland, Saaremaa, Gotland and Børnholm are ideal for exploring by bike. If you'd like to combine a cruise with a longer ride, the Turku Archipelago is perfect for a 4–5-day, easy-paced tour.

Canoeing/kayaking

Canoes and kayaks are a great way to see another side of a city and, in places like Oslo and the Stockholm Archipelago, the beauty of this clean, silent mode of travel can really be appreciated. Novices will probably prefer canoes (open) to kayaks (closed). Local companies hire all the gear and offer guided trips.

Ballooning

Stockholm is almost unique among major cities in that ballooning right over the city is permitted, providing a very special experience (*see p161*).

Skiing

In winter, great skiing at Tryvann Vinterpark is just a short metro ride from Oslo city centre. Holmenkollen has cross-country trails.

Children

It used to be relatively unusual to see children on a cruise ship, but this is no longer true. Most cruise companies today genuinely welcome youngsters. Still, it's always important to check before booking whether there are any age limits, and what facilities there are on board, though this last consideration may loom less large on a Baltic cruise, with its short and generally overnight passages.

On the other hand, it's pretty safe to say that the shore excursions offered with most cruises are definitely *not* tailored to children. Of course, some teenagers may be passionately interested in art galleries, cathedrals and museums, but most, and certainly most younger children, will get bored and fractious pretty quickly. For their sake, and possibly that of other passengers, you may well be advised to make your own arrangements while on shore. Here are some suggestions for attractions and diversions that will probably appeal to most children. However, you, and no one else, are the experts on your own offspring and only you can really judge what may appeal to them.

Open-air museums

The tangible re-creation of the past fascinates most youngsters, and if not, at least there's a bit more space to run around in. Examples listed in earlier pages include: Den Gamle By (Århus); Skansen (Stockholm); Seurasaari and Suomenlinna (Helsinki); Sjökvarteret (Mariehamn); Norsk Folkemuseum (Oslo); and those in Tallinn and Rīga. Another outdoor attraction that will enthrall many is Oslo's Vigelandsparken.

Amusement/theme parks

Examples already listed include Tivoli (Copenhagen) and Junibacken (Stockholm). Also try:

Linnanmäki (Helsinki), which is a traditional amusement park.
Tivolikuja 1 (just north of Töölonlahti). Tel: (035) 8977 399 600.
www.linnanmaki.fi

Moominworld is an island park based on the magical Moomin stories.
Naantali, near Turku. Tel: (0358) 2511 1111. www.muumimaailma.fi

Rīgas Cirks (Circus) is the only permanent circus in the Baltic. However, summer performances are less regular; the main season is October–April.
Merkela 4. Tel: (037) 6721 3279.
www.cirks.lv

Grona Lund amusement park, Djurgården, Stockholm

Zoos and aquaria

Mentioned in the main listings are Sjöfartsmuseet-Akvariet (Göteborg) and Akwarium Gdyńskie (Gdynia). There are well-run zoos in Copenhagen, Helsinki (Korkeasaari island), Tallinn and Rīga. Skansen (Stockholm) includes a small children's zoo, where domestic animals may be stroked. Also consider:

Sea Life Helsinki, *Tivolitie 10 (adjacent to Linnanmäki). Tel: (0358) 9565 8200. www.sealifeHelsinki.fi*

Aquaria Water Museum, *Falkenbergsgatan 2, Stockholm. Tel: (08) 660 9089. www.aquaria.se*

Museums

Some museums definitely will appeal to many kids, such as Vasamuseet (Stockholm); Vikingeskibsmuseet (Roskilde); Koggmuseet (Malmö); Nationalmuseet Children's Museum (Copenhagen); Vikingskipsmuseet, Frammuseet and Kon-Tiki Museet (Oslo). Also consider the great ships such as *Dar Pomorza* (Gdynia) and *Pommern* (Mariehamn). Many attractions do run special programmes for children, such as the Little Knights' Tour at Turun Linna (Turku Castle). Others to look at:

Experimentarium (Copenhagen), which is an exciting science-discovery centre. *Tuborg Havnevej 7 (Bus No 6 from Rådhuspladsen). Tel: (039) 27 33 33. www.experimentarium.dk*

Det Internasjonale Barnekunstmuseet (International Museum of Children's Art), Oslo, which features young people's art from almost every country in the world, and encourages participation. *Lille Frøens vei 4. Tel: (022) 46 85 73. www.barnekunst.no*

Cruising and cruise ships

Cruising has been the growth sector in the travel market in recent years, and as it has grown, so has it diversified. Old generalisations and preconceptions no longer stand up; the idea that cruising is the domain of well-heeled retired folk is long past its sell-by date.

Diversification has also led to specialisation. Now, for instance, some cruises target a young, party-oriented market, though more often in the Caribbean or Mediterranean than in the Baltic. This may change, but geography does count. Relatively short sailing distances mean that Baltic cruising is more focused on the onshore side of things. Not that the onboard experience is unimportant, but the balance is different, and Baltic cruising is generally more about the historical, cultural and natural richness of the region. This might suggest that it appeals more to the upper age range, but most Baltic cruises are on the short side (1–2 weeks), which enhances their appeal to a younger market.

Doing your homework

One attraction of cruising is its inclusivity; one payment covers transport, accommodation and at least the majority of meals. This does make it vitally important to check what

you're getting before you book. On a cruise ship you might have a choice of five restaurants and a couple of nightly entertainment programmes; in a city hotel, you'd have hundreds of options to choose from. There's plenty of choice within the Baltic cruise market, but you do make most of those choices before the voyage begins.

As you consider your choice of cruise, check exactly what is or isn't included in the price. You can usually assume that all meals are included when on board, but check whether you need to cover meals on days/nights in port. Check, too, whether excursions are included or charged separately.

Types of cruise ship

Cruising is more affordable than ever, and when you consider just how much is included, it can start to look like remarkably good value. Of course, not all cruises are created equal. While there's no standardised classification, there are some widely recognised categories.

Passengers disembarking from the *Crown Princess* in Oslo

De luxe/Ultra Luxury

De-luxe cruises operate smaller vessels (with usually 50–200 passengers). These provide very high levels of personal service, gourmet cuisine, and luxurious staterooms (the term 'cabin' is frowned upon), all with sea views. The upfront price is naturally steep but probably covers everything, including champagne at 3am if you feel like it. The number of crew will be almost equal to the number of passengers.

Luxury

Luxury vessels may be larger, but still retain high levels of personal service, approximately equivalent to a 5-star hotel. Again, all staterooms are sea facing. There are high standards of cuisine, usually from a choice of restaurants, and often guests will dress for dinner.

Premium

This is actually the commonest category of cruise and therefore the one with most variety. General standards of food and service approximately equate to a good 4-star hotel. There is considerable variation in the size of staterooms/cabins, and the cheapest are inside, with no natural light. The passenger:crew ratio will be 2:1 at best.

Standard

'Standard' cruise vessels may be older and lack some facilities that are increasingly expected – spas, saunas, swimming pools, live entertainers – and food is probably adequate rather than gourmet, but these cruises can be excellent value. And in the Baltic, where onshore time generally outweighs time on board, these frills may count for less anyway. Meals on board should still be included in the price, but do check in case you are expected to fend for yourself some evenings. As they're lower down the pecking order, these cruises may sometimes berth further from city centres.

Budget

It was easyJet founder Stelios Haji-Ioannou who devised the budget cruise. Unlike other cruises, the upfront price is on a room-only basis. Passengers pay as they go for meals, drinks, etc. It equates to a floating hotel, even a hostel in the cheapest cabins. At present easyCruise only operates in the eastern Mediterranean, but the concept has the potential to translate to the Baltic, with its short passages. Right now it is possible to mimic it on what we have called a 'DIY cruise' (*see pp24–5*) using scheduled ferries. Here, too, you pay as

you go for meals and drinks, and entertainment facilities are limited. The big difference is that DIY cruisers have to book each passage separately, possibly with different companies, and transfer their belongings between each leg of their journey.

Staterooms and cabins

Most cruise ships offer a broad range of accommodation, differentiated in the same way as hotel rooms, by size, facilities and outlook. Inevitably, the cheaper cabins will be compact, but good design should mean they don't feel cramped. Expect a shower but not a bath. Ten square metres (108sq ft) is a reasonable benchmark.

At the other extreme, large staterooms and suites will have king-size beds, sofas, walk-in wardrobes and a bath, plus turn-down service and the

A de-luxe stateroom on a Crystal cruise ship

other little touches you'd expect of a 5-star hotel. There will certainly be an outside view and possibly a balcony. Overall space may well be 40–50sq m (430–540sq ft).

A key distinction is between inside cabins and those with an ocean view. The design of modern cruise vessels maximises the number of outside cabins, but on larger vessels it's inevitable that some (perhaps a quarter to a third) of cabins will be inside.

On a typical Baltic cruise you spend little time in your cabin apart from sleeping, so this may not be a major disadvantage, unless you're prone to claustrophobia. Indeed, some people find the near-permanent daylight makes it hard to sleep, so an inside cabin could even be a plus!

Small is beautiful?

Cruise ships may carry 50 passengers, or over 3,000, though the real monsters are rarely seen in the Baltic. The smaller vessels are usually in the upper bracket, with exceptional personal service, though there's less choice in some respects; there may be only one restaurant, albeit a very good one. The larger vessels do offer more choice, and the chance for a change of scene.

Smaller ships, with their shallower draught, can go places the big ones can't. As well as visiting some smaller ports, they can often moor at the heart of the main cities, while the biggest ships are relegated to quays further away.

Shore excursions

As a rule, shore excursions are not included in the upfront price. There are exceptions, and excursions may also be thrown in as a special offer. The question is whether this actually does represent added value or not. These excursions have the advantage that everything's laid on, probably with a knowledgeable guide thrown in, but you may prefer to explore at your own pace, or seek out specific sites relevant to personal interests. Cruise brochures and websites give details of the excursions on offer. Study these and also read this guide and think about what you'd most like to see in each port.

You're encouraged to prebook excursions when you book your cruise. It may be possible to opt in when you're actually on board, and it certainly never hurts to ask, but this can't be guaranteed and you may be charged a premium. Conversely, if you book an excursion and then decide to opt out, you probably won't get a refund.

What to bring

On fly-cruises the 'fly' part limits the amount of baggage you can bring. On a cruise from the UK, or if you use surface transport to the departure port, there is no such restriction, but you will probably have to store everything within your cabin. DIY cruisers need to contend with transferring their belongings between ships, even between ports, and probably finding somewhere to store it during the day. For one reason or another, most cruise passengers need to keep their baggage within limits. This could be frustrating if you're keen to impress your fellow guests with a different outfit every night.

More practically, Baltic weather is variable. In high summer, daytime temperatures will usually stay above 20°C (68°F) and can get closer to 30°C (86°F), but every now and then a wind out of Lapland or Siberia can make it feel a lot colder. It is a fairly sunny region, but rain is always possible. Remember the wise words, attributed to everyone from John Ruskin to Billy Connolly: 'There is no such thing as bad weather, only inappropriate clothing.' So bring shorts and sandals, certainly, but also sturdy walking shoes, a fleece top and a lightweight waterproof. Perhaps the most useful item you can bring is a decent umbrella, one that packs away neatly but opens to a good size. And if you never need to open it, count it as a lucky charm.

One other thing to remember – when you set out, leave some spare capacity in your luggage. Very few people get through a Baltic cruise without buying a few items, whether they're the regular souvenirs or a handmade amber chess set, and you want to be able to pack them safely for your return home.

Cruise lines serving the Baltic region

English is the main language on board for these companies. Most are based in either the USA or UK but often have offices or agents elsewhere, and some have dedicated websites according to your country of origin. All the contact details here are for the UK, unless specified otherwise. Contact email addresses are given if the company publicises them.

For information about scheduled ferry services, *see p25*.

Azamara Club Cruises
www.azamaraclubcruises.com
North America *Tel: (1877) 999 9553.*
UK *Tel: 0800 018 2525.*
Email: infouk@rccl.com

Celebrity Cruises
www.celebritycruises.com
North America *Tel: (1800) 647 2251.*
UK *Contacts same as Azamara Cruises.*

Costa Cruises
www.costacruises.co.uk
Tel: 0845 351 0552.

Crystal Cruises
www.crystalcruises.com
Tel: (01888) 722 0021.

Cunard Cruises
www.cunard.com
Tel: 0845 071 3000.

Fred. Olsen Cruises
www.fredolsencruises.com
Tel: (0147) 3746 175.

Holland America Line
www.hollandamerica.com
Tel: 0845 351 0557.

MSC Cruises
www.msccruises.co.uk
Tel: 0844 561 7412.

Norwegian Cruise Line
www2.ncl.com
US *Tel: 0866 234 7350.*
UK *Tel: 0845 201 8900.*

P&O Cruises
www.pocruises.com
Tel: 0845 678 0014 (reservations).
Email: reservations@pocruises.com

Princess Cruises
www.princess.com
Tel: (0845) 355 5800.
Email: enquiry@princesscruises.co.uk

Regent Seven Seas
www.rssc.co.uk/rssc.com
US *Tel: (0877) 505 5370.*
UK *Tel: (0238) 068 2280.*

Royal Caribbean
North America *www.royalcaribbean.com*
Tel: (0800) 398 9819.
UK *www.royalcaribbean.co.uk*
Tel: 0844 493 4005.

Silversea Cruises
www.silversea.com
Australia & New Zealand
Tel: (061) 2 9255 0600.
North America
Tel: (0877) 760 9052.
UK *Tel: 0844 770 9030.*

Voyages of Discovery
North America
http://us.voyagesofdiscovery.com.
Tel: (0866) 623 2689.
Email: customerservice@
voyagesofdiscovery.com
UK *www.voyagesofdiscovery.co.uk.*
Tel: 0844 822 0802.
Email: info@voyagesofdiscovery.com

Cruising and cruise ships

Viking Line is a good option for those on a DIY cruise

Essentials

Arriving and departing

On cruises from the UK this is already taken care of anyway, and many fly-cruises will also include flight bookings. If travelling independently, Copenhagen is the easiest port to reach and is one of Europe's main air-hubs, with direct flights from six North American cities; Australasian travellers can connect through Dubai, Bangkok or Singapore. By train, London to Copenhagen (via Brussels and Cologne) takes about nineteen hours, Copenhagen to Stockholm five hours. There are direct flights from various UK and Republic of Ireland airports to Stockholm, Helsinki, Rīga, Tallinn, Gdańsk and Copenhagen. Low-cost airlines serving the Baltic include Ryanair, easyJet and Wizzair; SAS also has low fares. St Petersburg has regular flights to/from London and connections through Copenhagen, Helsinki, etc. From North America, connect through one of these hubs; from Australasia, Bangkok is the best bet.

Drinking water

Tap water should be safe to drink almost everywhere. It's reported that tap water in St Petersburg may contain the *giardia* parasite, though.

Electricity

Throughout the region the supply is 220–240V, 50Hz AC, and the plugs are the two round-pin type. UK and Australasian visitors will need a simple plug adaptor; North Americans will need a transformer.

Internet

Internet access is rarely hard to find, with Internet cafés in every city and many hotels offering Wi-Fi. St Petersburg lags a little here, but persistence soon pays off. Tallinn, by contrast, is bristling with hotspots.

Money

It's rarely difficult to find ATMs in the main cities, but they may be scarcer in some of the smaller places. Hotels and restaurants generally accept MasterCard and Visa; American Express cards are less widely accepted.

Finland, Germany and Estonia use the euro (divided into 100 cents). Lithuania is expected to follow suit in 2013. Latvia is also committed to joining but no date has been set. All three currencies, and the Danish krone, are pegged to the euro. The euro is often accepted in shops and restaurants here, and in Scandinavia, but always check first. Similarly, Danish kroner and Swedish kronor are often accepted in the other country, especially in Copenhagen and Malmö. In Russia, it is officially forbidden to use other currencies for cash payments.

Denmark: krone (100 øre)

Sweden: krona (100 öre)

Norway: krone (100 øre)
Poland: złoty (100 groszy)
Latvia: lat (100 santīmi)
Russia: ruble (100 kopecks)

Passports and visas

All visitors to Russia require a visa, which must be arranged in advance, and requires a visa support document. Cruise companies will take care of this, but your passport must be valid for at least six months beyond your date of departure from Russia. If travelling independently, *www.visatorussia.com* is a helpful site, or contact your Russian embassy.

None of the other countries require visas for stays under three months.

Pharmacies

Pharmacies, usually called *Apteek* or something similar (*see Language, pp152–5*) and indicated by an illuminated green cross, are widespread and run to high standards. Most pharmacists speak English.

Smoking

Smoking in restaurants and similar enclosed public places, usually including public transport, is now banned in eight of the ten countries. Poland has a partial ban (establishments can provide a separate room for smokers). Russia is currently the 'smokiest' country.

Telephones

British, Australian and New Zealand mobiles will normally work in the Baltic regions, provided your service contract allows roaming (check with your provider), and network coverage is almost 100 per cent. Most North American phones will *not* work, unless you have a triband phone.

Time

Norway, Sweden, Denmark, Germany and Poland are 1 hour ahead of GMT, 6 hours ahead of the eastern USA, 10 hours behind New Zealand; Finland, Lithuania, Latvia and Estonia are 2 hours ahead of GMT, 7 hours ahead of the eastern USA and 9 hours behind New Zealand; Baltic Russia is respectively 3 and 8 hours ahead and 8 hours behind New Zealand.

Toilets

In Germany and the Nordic countries toilets are reasonably widespread and very clean, but they may be expensive. In the former Eastern bloc, with the rapid growth in tourism, large numbers of portable toilets have been installed, often free but not always fragrant. In St Petersburg most are attended and clean, and a small charge is payable.

Travellers with disabilities

In Germany and the Nordic countries access is generally good. The former Eastern bloc lags some way behind but progress is being made. In St Petersburg, only major museums and high-end hotels are likely to meet 'Western' standards. The St Petersburg metro is emphatically not wheelchair accessible.

Language

In most of the cities around the Baltic, English is so widely spoken that you can get by without a word of any other language. In fact, if a German wants to talk to a Finn, or a Pole wants to chat with a Dane, they will normally do so in English. However, it still helps to be able to recognise common words and it's basic good manners to be able at least to say hello, please and thank you.

All the Baltic languages belong to the Indo-European family except Finnish and Estonian (*see p86*). Recognised sub-families are: West Germanic (includes German and English); North Germanic (Norwegian, Danish, Swedish); Baltic (Latvian, Lithuanian) and Slavic (Polish, Russian). The similarities between Polish and Russian are more apparent in spoken than written language because Russian uses a different alphabet, and for that reason is dealt with in more detail on *pp154–5*.

Sometimes the language itself isn't the only baffling thing – the alphabet can puzzle you, too

English	Danish	Norwegian	Swedish	German	Finnish	Estonian	Lithuanian	Latvian	Polish
Hello	Hej	Goddag	Hej, Goddag	Guten Tag	Hei	Tere, tervist	Labas	Sveiki	Dzień dobry
Good morning	God morgen	God morgen	God morgon	Guten Morgen	Hyvää huomenta	Tere hommikust	Labas rytas	Labrīt	Dzień dobry
Good afternoon	God eftermiddag	God ettermiddag	God middag	Guten Abend	Hyvää päivää	Tere päevast	Laba diena	Labdien	Dobry wieczór
Good evening	God aften	God kveld	God afton	Gute Nacht	Hyvää iltaa	Tere õhtust	Labas vakaras	Labvakar	Dobranoc
Goodbye	Farvel	Ha det bra	Adjö	Auf Wiedersehen	Näkemiin	Head aega	Viso gero	Uz redzēšanos	Do widzenia
Please	Vær så venlig	Vær så snill	Tack	Bitte	Ole hyvä	Palun	Prašau	Lūdzu	Proszę
Thank you	Tak	Takk	Tack	Danke	Kiitos	Tänan	Ačiū	Paldies	Dziękuję
Yes	Ja	Ja	Ja	Ja	Kyllä	Jah	Taip	Jā	Tak
No	Nej	Nei	Nej	Nein	Ei	Ei	Ne	Nē	Nie
Excuse me	Undskyld mig	Unnskyld meg	Ursäkta	Entschuldigen Sie	Anteeksi	Vabandage	Atsiprašau	Atvainojiet	Przepraszam
Entrance	Indgang	Inngang	Ingång	Eingang, Zugang	Sisään	Sissepääs	Įėjimas	Ieeja	Wejście
Exit	Udgang	Utgang	Utgång	Ausgang, Ausfahrt	Ulos	Väljapääs	Išėjimas	Izeja	Wyjście
Open	Åben	Åpen	Öppet	Offen	Avoinna	Avatud	Atdaras	Atvere	Otwarte
Closed	Lukket	Stengt	Stängt	Geschlossen	Suljettu	Suletud	Uždaras	Slēgts	Zamknięte
Railway station	Jernbanestation	Jernbanestasjon	Järnvägsstation	Bahnhof	Rautatieasema	Raudteejaam	Geležinkelio stotis	Dzelzceļa stacija	Dworzec kolejowy
Bus station	Rutebilstation	Busstasjon	Bussterminal	Busbahnhof	Linja-autoasema	Bussijaam	Autobusų stotis	Autoosta	Dworzec autobusowy
Metro	Metro	T-bane	T-bane	U-Bahn	Metro	n/a	n/a	n/a	n/a
Café	Kafé	Kafé	Kafé	Café	Kahvila	Kohvik	Kavinė	Kafejnīca	Kawiarnia
Restaurant	Restaurant	Restaurant	Restaurang	Restaurant	Ravintola	Restoran	Restoranas	Restorāns	Restauracja
Bar	Bar	Bar	Bar	Bar	Baari	Baar	Baras	Bārs	Baru
Coffee	Kaffe	Kaffe	Kaffe	Kaffee	Kahvi	Kohv	Kava	Kafija	Kawa
Tea	Te	Te	Te	Tee	Tee	Tee	Arbata	Tēja	Herbata
Beer	Øl	Øl	Öl	Bier	Olut	Õlu	Alus	Alus	Piwo
Cheers!	Skål!	Skål!	Skål!	Prost!	Kippis!	Terviseks!	Į sveikatą!	Priekā!	Na zdrowie!
Water	Vand	Vann	Vatten	Wasser	Vesi	Vesi	Vanduo	Ūdens	Woda
Toilet	Toiletter	Toalett	Toalett	Toilette	WC (vee-saa)	Tualett	Tualetas	Tualete	Toalety
Men	Herrer	Menn	Herrtoalett	Herren	Miehet	Meestele	Vyrų	Kungiem	Męska
Women	Damer	Kvinner	Damer	Damen	Naiset	Naistele	Moterų	Dāmām	Damska
Chemist	Apotek	Apotek	Apotek	Apotheke	Apteekki	Apteek	Vaistinė	Aptieka	Apteka
Doctor	Læge	Lege	Läkare	Arzt	Lääkäri	Arst	Gydytojas	Ārsts	Lekarz
Police	Politi	Politi	Polisen	Polizei	Poliisi	Politsei	Policija	Policija	Policja
Monday	Mandag	Mandag	Måndag	Montag	Maanantai	Esmaspäev	Pirmadienis	Pirmdiena	Poniedziałek
Tuesday	Tirsdag	Tirsdag	Tisdag	Dienstag	Tiistai	Teisipäev	Antradienis	Otrdiena	Wtorek
Wednesday	Onsdag	Onsdag	Onsdag	Mittwoch	Keskiviikko	Kolmapäev	Trečiadienis	Trešdiena	Środa
Thursday	Torsdag	Torsdag	Torsdag	Donnerstag	Torstai	Neljapäev	Ketvirtadienis	Ceturtdiena	Czwartek
Friday	Fredag	Fredag	Fredag	Freitag	Perjantai	Reede	Penktadienis	Piektdiena	Piątek
Saturday	Lørdag	Lørdag	Lördag	Samstag	Lauantai	Laupäev	Šeštadienis	Sestdiena	Sobota
Sunday	Søndag	Søndag	Söndag	Sonntag	Sunnuntai	Pühapäev	Sekmadienis	Svētdiena	Niedziela

RUSSIAN

It's worth devoting more space to Russian, for several reasons. One is that many cruises spend longer in St Petersburg than anywhere else. Another is that, although English is widely spoken in tourist areas, it's less universal than elsewhere. And third, the Cyrillic alphabet makes many words look alien when in fact they are quite familiar.

To take one (vital!) example. РЕСТОРАН might look baffling, but simply transliterating letters to their Roman equivalent turns it into RESTORAN. You can guess what that means, and you'd be right.

Cyrillic	Roman	Cyrillic	Roman
А а	a	Т т	t
Б б	b	У у	u
В в	v	Ф ф	f (or ph)
Г г	g	Х х	kh
Д д	d	Ц ц	ts
Е е	e	Ч ч	ch
Ё ё	e	Ш ш	sh
Ж ж	zh	Щ щ	shch
З з	z	Ы ы	y
И и	i	Э э	e
Й й	y	Ю ю	yu
К к	k	Я я	ya
Л л	l	Ъ ъ	hard signifier (affects
М м	m		how you pronounce
Н н	n		the preceding letter)
О о	o	Ь ь	soft signifier (affects
П п	p		how you pronounce
Р р	r		the preceding letter)
С с	s		

	Cyrillic form	Approximate pronunciation
Hello	Здравствуйте	zdravstvuitye
Good morning	Доброе утро	dobroe utro
Good afternoon	Добрый день	dobry den
Good evening	Добрый вечер	dobry vecher
Goodbye	До свидания	do svidaniya
Please	Пожалуйста	pozhalsta
Thank you	Спасибо	spasibo
Yes	Да	da
No	Нет	nyet
Excuse me	Простите	izvinitye
Entrance	Вход	vkhod
Exit	Выход	vykhod
Open	Открыто	otkryto
Closed	Закрыто	zakryto
Railway station	Вокзал	vokzal
Bus station	Автобусная станция	avtobusnaya stantsiya
Metro	Метро	metro
Café	Кафе	kafe
Restaurant	Ресторан	restoran
Bar	Бар	bar
Coffee	Кофе	kofe
Tea	Чай	chay
Beer	Пиво	pivo
Cheers!	За ваша здоровье!	za vasha zdorovye!
Water	Вода	voda
Toilet	Туалет	tualyet
Men	Мужская	muzhskaya
Women	Женщины	zhenshchiny
Chemist	Аптека	apteka
Doctor	Доктор	doktor
Police	Полиция	policiya
Monday	Понедельник	ponedyelnik
Tuesday	Вторник	vtornik
Wednesday	Среда	sreda
Thursday	Четверг	chetverg
Friday	Пятница	pyatnitsa
Saturday	Суббота	subbota
Sunday	Воскресенье	voskresenye

Emergencies

Emergency phone numbers

If using a mobile phone, *112* is the standard emergency number. It is also a standard emergency number from all phones in all the Baltic countries except Russia.

In several countries there is a separate number that dials directly to the police (for non-emergency calls):
Denmark *114*,
Estonia *110*,
Germany *110*,
Latvia *02*,
Poland *997*.

In Russia, the current numbers are:
Police *02*,
Ambulance *03*,
Fire *01*.
These are gradually changing to *112*.

If you are on an organised cruise, it is also wise to alert the crew on the cruise vessel immediately if you have an emergency; they will do all they can to help.

Health risks
On board

In general, there are few health risks when cruising in the Baltic. Hygiene standards on board ships are invariably high. In the very rare event of infection or food poisoning it will be dealt with very quickly, and in the Baltic you are never more than a few hours from port. Any such cases tend to make headlines, which can give an exaggerated impression of their frequency, but in reality you are no more at risk on board ship than in a high-standard hotel.

Onshore

Again, there are few major health issues for visitors to the Baltic region, and the usual common-sense precautions will minimise any risk. It may be prudent to avoid drinking tap water in St Petersburg though. In the summer, midges and mosquitoes can be an annoyance, more so in rural areas, but are only a serious risk to those rare individuals who react strongly to their bites. Winter visitors must be aware of the very low temperatures, certainly low enough to cause frostbite after prolonged exposure: wrap up warm, taking particular care of your hands, feet and head.

Medical services

British and Irish travellers can obtain free medical treatment in all countries except Russia; it is wise to carry a European Health Insurance Card (EHIC). Visit *www.ehic.org.uk* or call *0845 606 2030*. The card is free. To provide cover in Russia, you will need travel insurance. Travellers from non-EU countries will need insurance to cover all the countries visited. The

EHIC does not cover other potential costs, for which travel insurance is, of course, advised.

Safety and crime

Most of the Baltic cities are among the safest in the world; Helsinki, in particular, scores consistently highly in this regard, but Norway, Sweden, Denmark and Germany all have excellent records. Petty crime is slightly more prevalent in the Baltic republics and Poland, but with sensible precautions the risks remain minimal. Don't draw attention to yourself by wearing ostentatious jewellery or flashing large wads of cash, and avoid poorly lit areas, especially late at night. Carry cash and credit cards in a money-belt or secure inside pocket.

There are somewhat more reports of theft and occasional violent crime in St Petersburg. Pickpockets are active in crowded places, including on public transport. Still, most travellers will have no problems, especially if they follow the above precautions. Unfortunately, there have been reports of racist attacks by neo-Nazi skinheads, so travellers of Asian or African-Caribbean appearance should take extra care.

The Old Pharmacy in Tallinn

Directory

As this is a cruising guide, it may seem unnecessary to give accommodation listings for most ports. However, those undertaking fly-cruises or extending their trips may need accommodation in the turnaround ports, so a good range of accommodation is listed for Copenhagen and Stockholm. For the benefit of DIY cruisers, a few strategic hotels are also listed for other key ports.

Price guide

This guide covers ten different countries, with nine different currencies. There are wide differences in price levels, even before exchange-rate fluctuations are taken into account. It seems more helpful to indicate relative costs in the context of each destination and therefore, for both accommodation and dining, four price bands are used. In using these ratings, bear in mind that a half-decent pizza in Oslo may set you back as much as a good three-course meal in Rīga; similar comments apply to accommodation. Although these are relative price ratings, they are based on the cost of a typical meal without drinks, and on a typical double room. The prices of drinks in bars and restaurants may vary even more widely than those of food.

£	Budget
££	Moderate
£££	Moderately expensive
££££	Top end

SWEDEN

Stockholm

ACCOMMODATION

STF Hostel af Chapman & Skeppsholmen £
Hostel rooms (cabins) in the schooner *af Chapman*, moored opposite Gamla Stan; reception and more rooms in an attractive 18th-century building on land alongside. Great value, even without the atmospheric location.
Flaggemansvägen 8.
Tel: (08) 463 2266.
www.stfchapman.com

Gustav Vasa Hotel ££
Family-run hotel where every room is different; some have balconies and traditional tiled stoves. Close to Odenplan T-bana station.
Västmannagatan 61, Norrmalm.
Tel: (08) 343 801.
www.gustavvasahotel.se

Långholmen Hotel ££
Highly unusual hotel in a former prison; refurbished cells are small but comfortable, en-suite and with free Wi-Fi, and reasonably priced. Pleasant setting on wooded Långholmen.
Box 9116.
Tel: (08) 720 8500.
www.langholmen.com

Crystal Plaza ££–£££
Good location and a range of rooms from

spartan but good-value singles and doubles to tower rooms with abundant amenities and a suite with its own sauna.

Birger Jarlsgatan 35, Östermalm.

Tel: (08) 406 8800.

www.excellencehotels.se/crystalplaza

Clarion Collection Hotel Wellington £££

Cool, calm setting, close to Östermalmstorg T-bana station and handy for Djurgården. Comfortable rooms and nice extras – evening buffet included, free tea and coffee.

Storgatan 6, Östermalm.

Tel: (08) 667 0910.

www.choicehotels.no

Lady Hamilton £££

Small, welcoming, individualistic hotel in spot-on location. Folkloric décor, sauna and free Wi-Fi. 'Lady Rooms' service for solo female travellers.

Storkyrkobrinken 5, Gamla Stan.

Tel: (08) 506 40100.

www.lady-hamilton.se

Grand Hotel ££££

The Grand has seen more star names than most, and more Nobel Laureates than anywhere.

It has a magnificent location on the waterfront opposite Gamla Stan, and all the amenities of a true 5-star hotel. A legend.

Södra Blasieholmshamnen 8. Tel: (08) 679 3500.

www.grandhotel.se

EATING OUT

The best meal deals are usually at lunchtime, with generous buffets often at good prices. For inexpensive but wholesome food, head for a traditional market hall such as **Östermalms Saluhall** (T-bana Östermalmstorg) **£–££**, a fine 19th-century building crammed with food stalls, restaurants and cafés. Gamla Stan is full of eating-places, from basic to gourmet. Stockholmers are more likely to eat out in Norrmalm or Södermalm, where there are more mid-range options.

Chaikhana ££

Atmospheric tea room in the heart of Gamla Stan; great range of teas, plus good salads, sandwiches and cakes.

Svartmangatan 23, Skeppsholmen.

Tel: (08) 244 500.

www.chaikhana.se

Hermans ££

Good atmosphere, great views and terrific organic/vegetarian food: the buffets are top value.

Fjällgatan 23B, Södermalm.

Tel: (08) 643 9480.

www.hermans.se

Pelikan ££

Traditional Swedish home-style fare served in a historic panelled hall.

Blekingegatan 40, Södermalm.

Tel: (08) 556 09090.

www.pelikan.se

Ristorante Capri ££

Traditional, welcoming Italian restaurant in the city centre; generous, tasty pizzas and pasta dishes make it an excellent value choice.

Nybrogatan 15, Norrmalm.

Tel: (08) 662 3132.

Bistro Berns £££

Large, handsome restaurant facing a small park. Swedish and French influences in a menu that will delight meat-lovers but does little for vegetarians.

Berzeli Park, Norrmalm.
Tel: (08) 566 32200.
www.berns.se

Carl Michael £££
Named after troubadour
Carl Michael Bellman,
the restaurant has an
18th-century air and
focuses on classic
seasonal Swedish food.
Allmänna gränd 6,
Djurgården.
Tel: (08) 667 4596.
www.carlmichael.se

Eriks Gondolen £££
In the unique setting of a
cantilevered gantry,
Gondolen has possibly
the best views in
Stockholm, along with
sophisticated menus.
Stadsgården 6,
Södermalm.
Tel: (08) 641 7090.
www.eriks.se

Wedholms Fisk £££
This is one of the best
fish restaurants in
Stockholm. Menu
changes frequently to
reflect what's fresh.
Nybrokajen 17,
Norrmalm.
Tel: (08) 611 7874.
www.wedholmsfisk.se

Mathias Dahlgren ££££
Signature restaurant of
Bocuse d'Or winner in
the palatial Grand Hotel.

Top cuisine at prices
to match. Waterfront
views.
Södra Blasieholmshamnen
6, Blasieholmen.
Tel: (08) 679 3584.
www.mathiasdahlgren.com

ENTERTAINMENT

For entertainment and
nightlife, Stockholm is
not just the 'capital of
Scandinavia' but
probably of the entire
Baltic. Gamla Stan has
lots of traditional pubs.
Norrmalm has a
bewildering range of
bars, clubs and music
venues. On the edges of
Östermalm, Stureplan
has a clutch of bars and
clubs. Across in
Södermalm, the vibe is
generally young and
funky. Bars also
invariably serve some
sort of food.

Café Opera
As its name-dropping
website suggests, this
swanky bar/brasserie is
the place to see and be
seen in Stockholm.
There's a champagne
nightclub, too.
Operahuset, Norrmalm.
Tel: (08) 676 5807.
www.cafeopera.se

**Glenfiddich Warehouse
no.68**
Whisky specialist
(obviously) but also a
great place to find a
range of Swedish craft
beers.
Våsterlanggatan 68.
Tel: (08) 791 9090. www.
glenfiddichwarehouse.se

Järntorgspumpen
Comfortable pub for the
beer connoisseur.
Järntorget 83, Gamla
Stan. Tel: (08) 24 2400.

Jazzclub Fasching
Probably Stockholm's
leading jazz club, and a
key venue during the Jazz
Festival in July.
Kungsgatan 63.
Tel: (08) 534 82960.
www.fasching.se

Operan
The Royal Swedish
Opera stages the classic
opera repertoire and
hosts performances by
the Royal Swedish Ballet.
Gustav Adolfs Torg,
Norrmalm.
Tel: (08) 791 4400.
www.operan.se

SkyBar
Ninth-floor location at
the Radisson SAS Royal
Viking Hotel, by the
Central Railway Station,
means great views.

Vasagatan 1, Norrmalm.
Tel: (08) 506 54000.
Södra Teatern
Lavish old theatre and
studios present a wide
range of music, featuring
international names and
Swedish acts.
Mosebacke Torg 1–3,
Södermalm.
Tel: (08) 531 99400.
www.sodrateatern.com
Stockholms Konserthus
Blue concert hall, home to
the Royal Philharmonic
Orchestra. Also welcomes
visiting orchestras.
Hötorget 8, Norrmalm.
Tel: (08) 506 67788.
www.konserthuset.se
Wallmans Salonger
(Music venue)
Operator of several
venues including dinner
shows, musical theatres
and nightclubs.
www.wallmans.com

SPORT AND LEISURE
Bike & Hike (Cycling)
Guided bicycle rides on
Djurgården.
Tel: (0768) 165 529.
www.bikehike.se
Brunnsvikens
Kanotklubb (Canoeing)
Rents canoes and sea
kayaks at decent prices
(*May–Sept*).

Frescati Hagväg 5. Tel:
(08) 155 060. www.bkk.se
Far & Flyg (Ballooning)
Company with almost
30 years' experience.
Gröndalsvägen 38nb,
Gröndal. Tel: (08) 645
7700. www.farochflyg.se

Visby
EATING OUT
Bakfickan ££
Unpretentious and
popular seafood
restaurant at the heart of
Visby's Old Town.
Stora Torget 1.
Tel: (0498) 271 807.
www.bakfickan-visby.nu

Malmö
EATING OUT
Rådhuskällaren ££££
Top-notch restaurant in
the vaulted cellar of the
Town Hall. If the budget
won't stretch, there's a
wide choice nearby in
Stortorget and Lilla Torg.
Kompanigatan 5.
Tel: (040) 790 20.
www.profilrestauranger.se

FINLAND
Helsinki
ACCOMMODATION
Hotel Fabian ££
Stylish new boutique
hotel a couple of blocks

from Kauppatori.
Fabianinkatu 7.
Tel: (09) 6128 2000.
www.worldhotels.com
Hotel Helka ££
On the right side of the
centre for the cruise
terminals and handy for
tram and metro, Helka is
new, stylish and very
good value.
Pohjoinen Rautatiekatu
23. Tel: (09) 613 580.
www.helka.fi
Scandic Simonkenttä £££
Central modern hotel
with well-equipped,
spacious rooms.
Breakfast buffet.
Simonkatu 9.
Tel: (09) 68 380.
www.scandichotels.com

EATING OUT
In summer, open-air stalls
crowd Kauppatori
(Market Square) offering
everything from fresh
local fish to falafel. Nearby
Kauppahalli offers the
chance to assemble a
picnic, then hop on the
ferry to Suomenlinna and
eat overlooking the sea.
The Helsinki Menu label
indicates a set menu at
prices well below à la
carte at the same
establishment.

Café Chapman ££
By day a pleasant lunch spot with a sunny terrace, by night an à la carte restaurant. Set menus are good value.
Suomenlinna B1.
Tel: (09) 668 692.
www.chapman.fi

Café Ursula ££
Fabulous terrace looks over to Suomenlinna; perfect for coffee and cake, or a sandwich. Tempting evening menu with seafood prominent.
Ehrenströmintie 3 (edge of Kaivopuisto park).
Tel: (09) 652 817.
www.ursula.fi

Helka's Kitchen ££
In Hotel Helka (*see p161*). Offers a modern take on traditional Finnish cuisine.
Pohjoinen Rautatiekatu 23. Tel: (09) 6135 8672.
www.helka.fi

Havis ££–£££
Three restaurants in one (dining room, bistro and terrace) all specialising in fresh-caught seafood.
Eteläranta 16.
Tel: (09) 6128 5800.
www.royalravintolat.com

Fishmarket £££
Focuses on fresh fish, well prepared and served with style in attractive modern surroundings.
Pohjoisesplanadi 17.
Tel: (09) 1345 6220.
www.palacekamp.fi

Lasipalatsi £££
Striking 'glass palace' overlooking bustling Mannerheimintie. Renovated and extended in 2008. Menu features traditional Finnish favourites, with modern European influence. Good café downstairs.
Mannerheimintie 22–24.
Tel: (020) 742 4290. http:// ravintola.lasipalatsi.fi

Panimo Suomenlinna £££
Sample house beers in a vaulted dining room or flowery beer garden. Menu includes the likes of peppered noisettes of reindeer.
Rantakasarmi, Suomenlinna. Tel: (09) 228 5030. www.panimo.com

Turku
Accommodation
Centro Hotel ££
In a central yet tranquil St Petersburg-style courtyard. Rooms are small, but they don't feel cramped, and it's good value.
Yliopistonkatu 12A.
Tel: (02) 211 8100.
www.centrohotel.com

Naantali Spa Hotel ££££
Out of town, but if you're going to lovely Naantali, this is one of Finland's swankiest hotels, with the Sunborn Princess floating hotel alongside.
Matkailijantie 2.
Tel: (02) 445 50.
www.naantalispa.fi/ english/index.html

EATING OUT
As in Helsinki, the 100-year old Kauppahalli is the place to gather picnic ingredients, which could be eaten on the nearby waterfront. The Aura River is lined with floating restaurants.

Panimoravintola Koulu ££ (pub), £££ (restaurant)
Elegant former school (*koulu*) houses a brewery producing excellent beers. Ground floor has a pubby atmosphere and food, while upstairs is a smart à la carte restaurant. Large garden.
Eerkinkatu 18.
Tel: (02) 274 5757. www. panimoravintolakoulu.fi

Herman £££
Highly rated restaurant in attractive waterfront warehouse. 'Menu verte' is an excellent choice for vegetarians, and there's the TurkuMenu for the meat-eaters; both are great value.
Läntinen Rantakatu 37.
Tel: (02) 230 3333.
www.ravintolaherman.com

ENTERTAINMENT
Turku has several bars and restaurants in highly original premises.
Old Bank Public House
The fine Art Nouveau exterior is outdone by polished wood and brass inside.
Aurakatu 3. Tel: (02) 274 5700. www.oldbank.fi
Puutorin Vessa
Unusual pub in a former public lavatory. The exterior has protected status, while the interior is plain wacky.
Puutorintori.
Tel: (02) 233 8123.
www.puutorinvessa.fi
Uusi Apteeki
The name means 'old pharmacy'; many original fixtures remain. Finnish, Belgian, Irish and English beers.

Kaskenkatu 1.
Tel: (02) 250 2595.

SPORT AND LEISURE
Turku Touring (Cycling)
Complete archipelago cycling packages from June to mid-August.
Aurakatu 4, 20100 Turku.
Tel: (02) 262 7444.
www.turkutouring.fi

Mariehamn
ACCOMMODATION
Hotel Arkipelag £££
Modern hotel looking over Östra Hamnen and peaceful bay beyond. Spacious rooms.
Strandgatan 31.
Tel: (018) 24 020.
www.hotellarkipelag.com

EATING OUT
Pub Niska ££
Named after a notorious smuggler, with a nautical interior and a super waterfront terrace. Menu includes *plåtbröd*, a distinctive Åland take on the universal pizza.
Strandpromenaden.
Tel: (018) 19 141.
ÅSS Paviljongen £££
Centred on a handsome pavilion next door to, and allied with, Pub Niska. Fresh seasonal

produce prepared with a light touch.
Strandpromenaden, Västra Hamnen.
Tel: (018) 19 141.

ENTERTAINMENT
Hotel Arkipelag is where it's at in Mariehamn, with a dance restaurant, club and casino.

RUSSIA
St Petersburg
ACCOMMODATION
Rapid rise in demand for rooms has spawned lots of mini-hotels – some have just three rooms. Note: some hotels do not take non-Russian guests.
Arbat Nord ££
The 33 rooms are new and well equipped; location is reasonably central but will entail some walking (Chernevskaya Metro five minutes). Personal service makes it great value.
Artelleriyskaya ulitsa 4.
Tel: (812) 703 1899.
http://eng.arbat-nord.ru
Yards of Capella ££
Mini-hotel (ten rooms) tucked away in one of St Petersburg's famous 'yards'. Comfortable en-suite rooms with

traditional character, two blocks from Palace Square (*see p66*).

Enter from Bolshaya Konyushennaya 11 or Moika nab 20.

Tel: (812) 449 1790.

Angleterre ££££

Elegant, well-run hotel next to St Isaac's Cathedral, extensively renovated to international standards. Casino and nightclub on the premises. One of the better deals at the upper end of the market.

ul Malaya Morskaya 24.

Tel: (812) 494 5666.

www.angleterrehotel.com

EATING OUT

Blini Domik £

Blinis – Russian pancakes – cooked and served in seconds, with a wide choice of fillings.

Kolokolnaya ulitsa 8.

Tel: (812) 327 8979.

Stolle £

Cheap and cheerful chain specialising in *pirogi* (pies) – great value.

Several locations including: Konushenny pereulok 16.

Tel: (812) 312 1862.

www.stolle.ru

Yolki-Palki £

This restaurant chain, a smash in Moscow, has now reached St Petersburg. Success owes less to tacky 'Russian village' ambience, more to great value.

Nevskiy prospekt 88.

Tel: (812) 273 1594.

Grad Petrov/ Die Kneipe ££

Yes, it seems to have two names, but either way it's a find. The menu is German-influenced (sausages a speciality), with tasty in-house beers, including classic Hefeweizen.

Universitetskaya nab 5.

Tel: (812) 326 0137.

www.die-kneipe.ru

The Idiot ££

Dostoyevsky inspires this eccentric establishment. Try a 'Crime and Punishment' cocktail, browse the bookshelves (plenty of English titles) or beat the language barrier with a game of chess or backgammon. Food includes traditional Russian favourites. Good vegetarian options.

Moika 82.

Tel: (812) 315 1675.

James Cook ££

Vaulted cellar with a hint of English pub; the beer list is eclectic and the menu international. Free Wi-Fi.

Shvedsky pereulok 2, off Nevskiy prospekt.

Tel: (812) 312 3200.

Khutor Vodogray ££

Recreates a Ukrainian country inn (*khutor*) in central St Petersburg. Reasonably priced, robust, traditional food goes down well with dark Ukrainian beer.

Karavannaya 2.

Tel: (812) 570 5737.

Na Zdorovie ££

The name is Russian for 'cheers'. The restaurant has a colourful rustic feel and does nicely dressed Russian favourites from *borscht* to chicken Kiev.

Bolshoy prospekt 13.

Tel: (812) 232 4039.

www.concord-catering.ru

Tinkoff ££

Large brew-pub (St Petersburg's first) with sleek, stylish interior. Menu features *borscht*, pasta, pizza and a range of steaks. Very busy at weekends.

Kazanskaya ulitsa 7.
Tel: (812) 118 5566.
Magrib £££
The name's Middle
Eastern and there's
shashlik on the menu,
but this is no cheap
kebab joint. There's a
grandly vaulted dining
room, meat comes
all the way from Libya,
and the menu is
cosmopolitan.
Nevskiy prospekt 84.
Tel: (812) 275 7620.
Palkin ££££
Dating back over 200
years, this is possibly
St Petersburg's most
famous restaurant and
one of its best. Priccy, so
why not really splash out
and try the sterlet
sturgeon baked in white
wine. Live music in the
main dining room.
Nevskiy prospekt 47, two
blocks east of Fontanka
River.
Tel: (812) 703 5371.
www.palkin.ru/eng

ENTERTAINMENT
Mariinsky Theatre
A palatial theatre built
in 1860, home to
legendary opera and ballet
companies. The repertoire
is dominated by the
classics, such as
Tchaikovsky's *Eugene*
Onegin and *Swan Lake*,
along with Mozart, Verdi
and Rossini.
Teatralnaya pl 1.
Tel: (812) 326 4141.
www.mariinsky.ru/en.
Also has a Concert Hall at
Pisarev ul 20.

St Petersburg State Jazz
Philharmonic Hall
A relatively recent
foundation (1989),
financed by the State
but built on Russia's
deep jazz traditions,
the hall hosts regular
shows by the Jazz
Philharmonic and by
many visiting artists. The
smaller Ellington Hall is
more like a traditional
jazz club.
Zagorodnyi prospekt 27.
Tel: (812) 764 8565.
www.jazz-hall.spb.ru
St Petersburg
Philharmonia
This magnificent concert
hall dating from 1839
provides a glittering
setting for regular
concerts by both the
Philharmonic and the
Academic Symphony
Orchestras, plus visiting
artists. There's also a
smaller hall on Nevskiy
Prospekt, ideal for
chamber music.
Grand Hall:
Mikhailovskaya 2.
Tel: (812) 312 9871.
Small Hall: Nevskiy
prospekt 30.
Tel: (812) 312 4585.
www.philharmonia.spb.ru

SPORT AND LEISURE
Nevskiye Bani
Banya is the Russian
equivalent of a sauna,
with a hint of the
Middle Eastern
hammam. Lie down and
get your 'banya buddy'
to thrash you with birch
twigs…
ul. Marata 5–7.
Tel: (812) 311 1400.

ESTONIA
Tallinn
ACCOMMODATION
Meriton Old Town
Hotel £££
At the end of Vanalinn
nearest the cruise
terminal, this 41-room
hotel offers a historic
atmosphere combined
with modern
convenience and
excellent service.
Lai 49.
Tel: (0372) 614 1300.
www.meritonhotels.com

Tallink City Hotel £££

Steely modern exterior, feels light years from Vanalinn, but it's barely five minutes' walk. Spacious rooms and all mod cons.

A Laikmaa 5.
Tel: (02) 630 0800.
http://hotels.tallink.com

EATING OUT

Beer House ££

Tallinn's only brew-pub, producing unpasteurised, unadulterated beer. Food is straightforward and robust. The interior is reminiscent of a Bavarian *Bierkeller* and the terrace stretches a long way down the street.

Dunkri 5.
Tel: (02) 581 96670.
www.beerhouse.ee

Café Mademoiselle ££

Attached to the Meriton Old Town Hotel, this is a comfortable café on a quiet street. There's another branch at the Meriton Grand downtown, whose in-house bakery produces some of the best cakes in Tallinn.

Lai 49.
Tel: (02) 614 1350.
www.meritonhotels.com

Restaurant City (in Tallink City Hotel) ££

A good city-centre choice, only five minutes' walk from the Viru gate. Inclusive buffets are good value, especially at lunchtime. Highly rated à la carte restaurant.

A Laikmaa 5.
Tel: (02) 630 0818.
www.hotels.tallink.com

Kaerajaan £££

Kaerajaan fuses Estonian tradition with modern cuisine; results are intriguing and delicious. Interior is sharp but comfortable and the terrace catches the last of the evening sun. Excellent value, too.

Raekoja plats 17.
Tel: (02) 615 5400.
www.kaerajaan.ee/eng

Kloostri Ait £££

A handsome fireplace and an antique piano are key features. Good for snacks, lunches, steaks and succulent home-baked bread. Live jazz most weekends.

Vene tänav 14.
Tel: (02) 641 8374.
www.kloostriait.ee

Olde Hansa £££

The medieval Olde Hansa, just off Raekoja plats, is Tallinn's best-known restaurant. Purists may question its authenticity, but it's a lot of fun and the candlelit interior is stunningly real. The food is rich and the dark spiced beer is a great accompaniment. Live medieval music, too.

Vana turg 1.
Tel: (02) 627 9020.
www.oldehansa.com

Balthasar ££££

Just off Raekoja plats, Balthasar specialises in the creative use of garlic (yes, even in desserts). There are alternatives for the faint-hearted.

Raekoja plats 11.
Tel: (02) 627 6400.
www.balthasar.ee

Karl Friedrich ££££

Of the many and various restaurants around Raekoja plats, this is probably the most distinguished. Fine dining upstairs, with a more 'pubby' cellar.

Raekoja plats 5.
Tel: (02) 627 2413.
www.karlfriedrich.ee.

ENTERTAINMENT

Estonian National Opera
Imposing classical opera house stages wide range of opera, ballet, musicals and more.
Estonia pst 4.
Tel: (372) 683 1260.
www.opera.ee.

Song Grounds
The vast stage and its surrounding grounds is the setting for the national Song Festival, as well as pop, rock and classical concerts.
Narva maantee 95.
Tel: (02) 611 2102.

Saku Suurhall
Tallinn's largest indoor venue features basketball, ballroom dancing and concerts from artists of the stature of Sting.
Paldiski Mnt 104B.
Tel: (06) 600 201.

Saaremaa

ACCOMMODATION

Repo Hotell ££
Charming old building in Kuressaare Old Town with 14 rooms, all en-suite.
Vallimaa 1a.
Tel: (045) 3 3510.
www.saaremaa.ee/repo/eng.htm

LATVIA

Rīga

ACCOMMODATION

Islande Hotel £££
Competent modern hotel on Kipsala island: many rooms enjoy a fine view to Vecrīga.
Kipsalas iela 20.
Tel: (02) 6760 8000.
www.islandehotel.lv

Konventa Seta £££
Hotel in a veritable warren of a former convent, in the heart of Vecrīga. Full of character.
Kaleju iela. 9/11.
Tel: (02) 6708 7501.
www.konventa.lv

EATING OUT

Dzirnavas £
Cheap, cheerful and authentic, this pulsatingly popular self-service restaurant is the antithesis of Old Town whimsy.
Dzirnavaiela 76.
Tel: (02) 6728 6204.

Mīvatnas vēji £££
Grill-bar on the roof of Islande Hotel has a great view to Vecrīga – wonderful on summer evenings. Fresh dishes are prepared right beside the bar. Good value considering its location.
Kipsalas iela 20.
Tel: (02) 6760 8000.
www.islandehotel.lv

Taverna Dzintara Cela (Amber Way Tavern) £££
Atmospheric vaulted basement in the Jēkaba Kazarmas (Jacob's Barracks). Good traditional food and beer with friendly service. Occasional live music.
4 Torņu iela.
Tel: (02) 732 1260.

Salve ££££
Salve offers traditional local delicacies and international favourites. A seven-course tasting menu offers Latvian specialities like fried pike-perch with celeriac mash and quince sauce.
Ratslaukums 5.
Tel: (02) 6704 4317.
www.salverestaurant.lv

LITHUANIA

Klaipėda

EATING OUT

Čili Kaimas ££
Family restaurant in old Soviet-era cinema: good-value standard menu includes lots of seafood.
H Manto 11. Tel: (0846) 310 953. www.cili.lt

Memelis ££

Brewery restaurant in a riverside warehouse, offering distinctive beers and strongly Lithuanian menu. Club upstairs.
Žvejų 4.
Tel: (0846) 403 040.
www.memelis.lt

Būrų Užeiga (Būrai Pub) £££

Taste the authenticity at this Old Town restaurant with wood-lined interior, serving traditional Lithuanian favourites.
Kepėjų 17.
Tel: (0846) 411 319.

SPORT AND LEISURE

Cycling

Kuršių Nerija (Curonian Spit) is ideal for two-wheeled exploration – for bike hire enquire at the main tourist office.
Turgaus g 7.
Tel: (0846) 412 186.

POLAND

Gdynia and Gdańsk

EATING OUT

Pierogarnia U Dzilea ££

The place to go for *pierogi*, with a wide range of fillings. If that's not your thing, there are other meat and fish dishes, too.
ul Piwna 59/60.
Tel: (058) 305 26 76.

Brovarnia Gdansk £££

Fine beer brewed right behind the bar is backed up by good pubby grub, or there's a more formal restaurant upstairs. Sunny terrace, too.
ul Szafarnia 9.
Tel: (058) 320 19 70.
www.brovarnia.pl

Czerwone Drzwi £££

Homely atmosphere in an old burgher's house near St Mary's Church; drop in for coffee by day or savour excellent seasonal food later on (booking advised).
ul Piwna 52/53, Gdańsk.
Tel: (058) 301 57 64.
www.reddoor.gd.pl

Róża Wiatrów £££

Next to *Dar Pomorza*, this huge restaurant caters efficiently for families, large groups and everyone else. Live music often features in the main dining room.
Al Jana Pawła II 2, Gdynia.
Tel: (058) 620 32 53.
www.rozawiatrow.com.pl

Pod Łososiem ££££

Gdańsk's most famous restaurant. Opulent interior matches contemporary take on traditional dishes.
ul Szeroka 54, Gdańsk.
Tel: (058) 301 76 52.
www.podlososiem.com.pl

GERMANY

Rostock

EATING OUT

Ratskeller Rostock £££

All around the Baltic, Town Hall cellars seem to be good places to eat, and this is no exception. Good steaks, nice atmosphere.
Neuer Markt.
Tel: (0381) 510 84 60.
www.ratskeller-rostock.de

Lübeck

EATING OUT

Café Niederegger ££

A must for lovers of marzipan, with an informative 'marzipan salon' and 12 life-size marzipan figures. Marzipan nut cake and marzipan cappuccino are popular.
Breite Strasse 89.
Tel: (0451) 530 11 26.
www.niederegger.de

Ratskeller ££££

Handsome vaulted cellar serving regional specialities; groups can try the Buddenbrooks Menu.

Markt 13.

Tel: (0451) 720 44. www. ratskeller-zu-luebeck.de

DENMARK
Copenhagen
ACCOMMODATION

Hotel Joergensen £

Hotel-cum-hostel, with singles, doubles, family rooms and dormitories. Simple en-suite rooms are one of the best deals in town.

Roemersgade 11.

Tel: (033) 13 81 86.

www.hoteljoergensen.dk

Ibsens ££

Converted apartment block in quiet area, with pétanque pitch in the courtyard. Rooms are all en-suite, ranging from simple to spacious.

Vendersgade 23.

Tel: (033) 13 19 13.

www.ibsenshotel.dk

Saga Hotel ££

Very near Central Station, this family-run hotel in a 19th-century apartment building has bright, clean and good value rooms.

Colbjørnsensgade 18.

Tel: (033) 24 49 44.

www.sagahotel.dk

Bertrams Hotel Guldsmeden £££

Balinese influence permeates the stylish décor, with four-poster beds and original artworks. Organic breakfast menu and bathroom supplies.

Vesterbrogade 107.

Tel: (070) 208 107.

www.hotelguldsmeden.dk

Best Western Hotel Hebron £££

Centrally located in an elegant building with spacious rooms. Free Wi-Fi and tea/coffee-making facilities in all rooms.

Helgolandsgade 4.

Tel: (033) 31 69 06.

www.hebron.dk

Comfort Hotel £££

Attractive building from 1891: elegant high-ceilinged rooms. Good location close to Kastellet, Den Lille Havfrue and cruise terminals.

Esplanaden. Bredgade 78.

Tel: (033) 48 10 00.

www.choicehotels.no

Danmark £££

On the corner of Rådhuspladsen, so super-central, but a quiet courtyard lends a sense

of calm. It's part of a small group claiming to be the world's first CO_2-neutral hotel chain.

Vester Voldgade 89.

Tel: (033) 11 48 06.

www.hotel-danmark.dk

Imperial Hotel £££

Large, efficiently run hotel near Central Railway Station (and right next to Vesterport for local trains); rooms are well laid out, staff are friendly and helpful.

Vester Farimagsgade 9.

Tel: (033) 12 80 00.

www.imperial-hotel-copenhagen.com

Scandic Copenhagen £££

Unlovely tower-block exterior, but most rooms have good views, and all have desks and Wi-Fi. Good location by lake, close to Central Station.

Vester Søgade 6.

Tel: (033) 14 35 35.

www.scandichotels.com/en

Hotel Admiral ££££

Fantastic location on the waterfront near Royal Playhouse and looking across to Operaen, with wooden sailing ships often moored outside. The listed building (1787) oozes atmosphere, with exposed beams in most rooms.

Toldbodgade 24.
Tel: (033) 74 14 14.
www.admiralhotel.dk

Hotel Alexandra ££££

Green Key certification signifies good environmental practice at this comfortable hotel, which features classic Danish furniture. One floor is declared 100 per cent allergy-proof.

H C Andersens
Boulevard 8.
Tel: (033) 74 44 44.
www.hotel-alexandra.dk

EATING OUT

Tivoli has 38 different restaurants and fast-food booths. Notable are the Viking-themed **Restaurant Valhal ££**, serving suitably hearty meat dishes washed down with mead, and **Færgekroen Bryghus £££**, a waterside pub that brews its own beer. The north side of Nyhavn is lined with restaurants – see below for choices, or stroll along during the day and study menus to make a choice for the evening. The Latin Quarter (north of Strøget) is good for unpretentious, good value eating.

Husmandskost on menu or placard suggests traditional, homely Danish dishes, usually filling and cheap.

Riz Raz £

A popular Middle Eastern restaurant between Strøget and Slotsholmen, its lunchtime and evening buffets are one of the best-value offerings in town. An excellent choice for vegetarians.

Kompagnistræde 20.
Tel: (033) 15 05 75.
www.rizraz.dk.

Ad Libitum ££

An 'all you can eat' buffet restaurant, with a wide-ranging choice of Nordic and Mediterranean dishes. For the hearty appetite, this could the best deal in Copenhagen. Groups pay by the hour.

Axeltorv 3.
Tel: (033) 13 27 47.
www.adlibitum-kbh.dk

Café Sommerhuset ££

Summer café and restaurant handy for cruise terminals. Food is simple but well-prepared (salads, burgers, steaks, homemade ice cream).

Churchillparken 7.
Tel: (033) 32 13 14.

Bistro Boheme £££

Specialising in cocktails, and with a terrific beer list, it's a great place for a drink. If you also want to eat, the menu is fresh and original.

Esplanaden 8.
Tel: (033) 93 98 44.
www.bistroboheme.dk

Brasserie Imperial £££

Traditional French/ international dishes dominate but there's always a traditional Danish dish, which changes daily and is good value.

Vester Farimagsgade 9.
Tel: (033) 43 23 83.
www.brasserieimperial.dk

Cap Horn £££

Classic Nyhavn restaurant with many original features, giving a quirky and relaxed ambience. The menu is fresh and contemporary, with a strong emphasis on organic ingredients.

Nyhavn 21.
Tel: (033) 12 85 04.
www.caphorn.dk

Café Sari £££
Small atmospheric place in an attractive square just off Strøget. Good lunches with excellent *smørrebrød*, sophisticated modern evening menu.
Nytorv 5.
Tel: (033) 14 84 55.
www.cafesari.dk

Ida Davidsen £££
Weekdays only, closes 4pm. Far from a 'sandwich bar', it's a temple to *smørrebrød*, with one of the longest menus you'll ever see.
Store Kongensgaade 70.
Tel: (033) 91 36 55.
www.idadavidsen.dk

Vesterbro Bryghus £££
Close to Rådhuspladsen and Tivoli, this establishment brews excellent beers (lagers, ales and a wheat beer) and serves hearty fare: try lamb shank braised in beer.
Vesterbrogade 2B.
Tel: (033) 11 17 05.
www.vesterbrobryghus.dk

Restaurant
Geranium ££££
Michelin-starred restaurant in the lovely setting of Kongens Have, run by two young chefs dedicated to organic and biodynamic food and wine, and making original use of fresh seasonal produce.
Kongens Have,
Kronprinsessegade 13.
Tel: (033) 11 13 04.

ENTERTAINMENT
Copenhagen is big on nightlife, in the truest sense. Many venues only hit their stride after midnight: truly dedicated funsters warm up in trendy pre-club bars. It's a fast-changing market, so check out the latest listings from the **Copenhagen Right Now** visitor centre or *www.visitcopenhagen.com*

Beer lovers are well catered for, with several brewery restaurants (*see restaurant listings for a couple of suggestions*).

Bar Rouge
The minimalistic bar at the 5-star Hotel Sankt Petri has resident DJs playing jazz and funk at the weekend, plus some of the best bartenders in town, who make mixing cocktails almost an art form.
Krystalgade 22.
Tel: (033) 45 98 22.
www.sktpetri.com

Castle Concerts
Free concerts in various historic venues around København (Wed 5pm).
Tel: (033) 25 74 00.
www.castleconcerts.dk

Den Glade Gris
Youthful hangout with long vaulted bar and upstairs disco. The name means 'The Happy Pig'.
Lille Kannikestræde 3.
Tel: (033) 32 96 97.
www.dengladegris.com

KB-Hallen
A leading rock venue, promoting the likes of Deep Purple, Duran Duran and Ice Cube.
Peter Bangs Vej 147,
Frederiksberg.
Tel: (038) 71 41 50.
www.kbhallen.dk

Koncerthuset
Brand-new concert hall, opened in January 2009. Its programme of concerts crosses genres, from symphony and choral to rock, pop, jazz and chamber music.
Emil Holms Kanal 20.
Tel: (035) 20 20 30.
www.dr.dk/Koncerthuset

La Fontaine

The city's oldest jazz club has hosted some legendary jam sessions.
Kompagnistræde 11.
Tel: (033) 11 60 98.
www.lafontaine.dk

Mojo Blues Bar

Top venue for blues, plus soul, rock, zydeco, bluegrass, with live music every night.
Løngangstræde 21.
Tel: (033) 11 64 53.
www.mojo.dk

Ølbaren

The name simply means 'beer-bar'. No Carlsberg or Tuborg but a terrific range of character beers from Denmark, Belgium, Germany and beyond.
Elmegade 2.
Tel: (035) 35 45 34.
http://oelbaren.dk

Operaen (Opera House)

A world-class venue for opera, ballet, orchestral and choral music.
Ekvipagemestervej 10.
Ticket hotline.
Tel: (033) 69 69 69.
www.operaen.dk

Rundetaarn (The Round Tower)

The library hall provides an unusual, atmospheric venue for small-scale performances such as chamber music recitals.
Købmagergade 52a.
Tel: (033) 73 03 73.
www.rundetaarn.dk

Søpavillonen

Fanciful lakeside pavilion, live music mostly from 1980s tribute bands.
Gyldenløvesgade 24.
Tel: (033) 15 12 24.
www.sopavilionen.dk

Tivoli Concert Hall

Well-regarded acoustics, with visits from the likes of k d lang or the New York City Ballet, and an annual Tivoli International Piano Competition.
Tel: (033) 15 10 12.
www.tivoli.dk

SPORT AND LEISURE

Bike Copenhagen with Mike

Guided tours (always in English) with enthusiastic and knowledgeable guide.
Turesensgade 10.
Tel: (026) 39 56 88. www.bikecopenhagenwithmike.dk

KajakOle

Kayak tours in exceptionally stable, unsinkable boats around the canals of Copenhagen.
Strandgade 50, 1401 Copenhagen K.
Tel: (040) 50 40 06.
http://kajakole.com

Århus

EATING OUT

Café Grene £

This café attached to an eclectic discount store does tasty organic food and great coffee.
Søndergade 11.
Tel: (086) 14 97 44.

Restaurant Terrassen ££

A beautiful wooden pavilion, built in 1904 and faithfully restored, makes a wonderful setting. The menu offers contemporary Danish cuisine at reasonable prices.
Skovbrynet 1 (entrance through Tivoli Friheden amusement park. Private entrance from Skovbrynet when park is closed).
Tel: (086) 14 29 00. www.restaurantterrassen.dk

Restaurant Navigator £££

On the waterfront with a great view across Århus Bay, this restaurant is, unsurprisingly, strong on seafood. The adjacent

Sailor's Pub is a cosy place for a drink.
Marselisborg Havnevej 46D. Tel: (086) 20 20 58.
www.rest-navigator.dk

Entertainment
Train
One of Denmark's leading music venues for rock, pop, blues, jazz, Train regularly hosts international names. Discount admission with an AarhusCard. The attached Kupé bar-lounge also has regular live music and DJs.
Toldbodgade 6.
Tel: (086) 13 47 22.
www.train.dk

Roskilde
Eating out
Raadhuskælderen £££
Good lunchtime sandwiches, nice evening menu, including dishes such as Bornholm chicken breast stuffed with truffles.
Fondens bro 3.
Tel: (046) 36 01 00.
www.raadhuskaelderen.dk

Sport and leisure
Canoe Rental
Paddle a kayak on peaceful Roskilde fjord.

Blodhøjvej 2, 4040 Jyllinge.
Tel: (046) 73 43 50.
www.outdoor-company.dk

NORWAY
Oslo
Eating out
Deli de Luca £
Deli de Luca is several cuts above your average fast food place, with thoroughly palatable pasta, calzones, fresh salads, nice cakes and good coffee. Most branches have a simple seating area.
Branches throughout the city.

Peppes Pizza ££
Another solid choice for those on a budget; comfortable restaurants specialising in well-made pizzas – choose from proper Italian-style pizza or American 'pizza pie'.
Branches throughout the city. www.peppes.no

Saras Telt ££
'Telt' means 'tent', but the canopies are pretty solid. Food and drink is good, straightforward fare and reasonably priced.
Karl Johans gate 24.
Tel: (022) 41 78 27.

Theatercaféen £££
This elegant Viennese-style café is an Oslo institution. Great coffee, cakes and sandwiches by day; brasserie-style meals (reservations advised) by night.
Stortingsgaten.
Tel: (022) 82 40 00.
www.theatercaféen.no

Lofoten Fiskerestaurant ££££
Lofoten lies at the far end of Aker Brygge but still pulls in the punters. It might be the view, or the exquisitely fresh fish and shellfish on offer.
Stranden 75. Tel: (022) 83 08 08. www.lofoten-fiskerestaurant.no

Entertainment
Zinatra Karaoke og Musikkbar
You don't need to speak Norwegian to translate the name.
Holmensgt 4, Aker Brygge.
Tel: (022) 83 07 02.
Open: Tue–Sat.

Sport and leisure
Cycling
Bike hire from Skiservice at Holmenkollen.
Tel: (022) 13 95 00.
www.skiservice.no

Index

Acknowledgements

Thomas Cook Publishing wishes to thank JON SPARKS, to whom the copyright belongs, for the photographs in this book, except for the following images:

CRYSTAL CRUISES 146
DANISH TOURIST BOARD 118, 119
DREAMSTIME.COM 98 (Jaroslaw Grudzinski)
FOTOLIA 68 (Galina Moiseeva)
WIKIMEDIA COMMONS 29 (Dirk Schröder), 86 (Sabine Hack), 87 (Mannobult), 97 (Marcin Sochacki), 99 (Brosen), 101 (Michael Paul Grollmer), 102 (Arnold Paul), 103 (Jorges)
WWW.LITHUANIANTRAVEL.LT 94 (K Driskius)

For CAMBRIDGE PUBLISHING MANAGEMENT LIMITED:
Project editor: Rosalind Munro
Typesetter: Paul Queripel
Proofreaders: Emma Haigh & Michele Greenbank
Indexer: Karolin Thomas

SEND YOUR THOUGHTS TO
BOOKS@THOMASCOOK.COM

We're committed to providing the very best up-to-date information in our travel guides and constantly strive to make them as useful as they can be. You can help us to improve future editions by letting us have your feedback. If you've made a wonderful discovery on your travels that we don't already feature, if you'd like to inform us about recent changes to anything that we do include, or if you simply want to let us know your thoughts about this guidebook and how we can make it even better – we'd love to hear from you.

Send us ideas, discoveries and recommendations today and then look out for your valuable input in the next edition of this title.

Emails to the above address, or letters to the traveller guides Series Editor, Thomas Cook Publishing, PO Box 227, Coningsby Road, Peterborough PE3 8SB, UK.

Please don't forget to let us know which title your feedback refers to!